SINGULARITY AND ROBOTICS

The Awakening of Artificial
Intelligence From the

Laboratory to the Real World

Pedro Agüero Vallejo

DEDICATION:

To Ynocencia Fernández de Agüero,

Marlene Lioced, Jeffrey Bienvenido,

Pedro Joel Agüero.

Index

Introduction

At the dawn of a new millennium, we find ourselves amidst a technological revolution that is irrevocably transforming our society, economy, and worldview. Advances in areas such as artificial intelligence and robotics drive this revolution—technologies that once belonged to the realm of science fiction but are now a tangible and growing reality.

(Singularity and Robotics: The Awakening of Artificial Intelligence. From the Laboratory to the Real World) aims to explore this fascinating and challenging technological landscape. Through its pages, we will embark on a journey that begins in high-tech laboratories where the latest innovations in artificial intelligence and robotics are being forged, and it will lead us to a near future where these technologies could be integrated into every aspect of our daily lives.

However, this book is not just a tour of technological wonders in the present and the future. It is also a reflection on what these advances mean for us as a society and as individuals. What will happen when machines can perform all the tasks that humans currently do, and possibly do them better? How will we adapt to a world where artificial intelligence is omnipresent? And, what happens when we reach singularity, the theoretical point at which machines surpass human intelligence?

These are complex and challenging questions, and I do not claim to have all the answers. However, my hope is that by exploring these topics, we can begin to better understand the era of artificial intelligence and robotics into which we are entering and chart a path toward a future where humanity and machines can coexist and thrive together. Welcome to the journey toward singularity.

Chapter 1:

Awakening of Artificial Intelligence

The term "Awakening of Artificial Intelligence" suggests the birth and rapid evolution of this transformative technology that is fundamentally changing the way human societies function. However, this "awakening" is not a singular event but a continuous process of development and refinement.

Artificial intelligence (AI) refers to the ability of a computing system to perform tasks that typically require human intelligence, such as learning, perception, decision-making, natural language processing, and problem-solving. AI systems can learn from experience, adjust their responses to new inputs, and perform tasks similar to those of humans. However, unlike humans, AI systems can process and analyze vast amounts of information at incredibly high speeds.

The "awakening" of AI is a metaphor for its ascent from theoretical concepts to the practical applications we have today. Starting from the second half of the 20th century, with the advent of computers and programming techniques, AI began to take shape. In recent decades, with the rise of cloud computing, big data, and advanced algorithms, AI has undergone an "awakening," transitioning from an academic curiosity to becoming an integral part of our daily lives.

Delving into the Understanding of the Concept: Awakening of Artificial Intelligence

To understand the concept of the "Awakening of Artificial Intelligence" (AI), we must first define what we mean by Artificial Intelligence. In general terms, AI refers to the simulation of human intelligence in machines that are programmed to think like humans and replicate their actions. AI can be categorized as weak or strong; weak AI refers to systems designed and trained for a specific task (such as personal voice assistants), while strong AI, also known as general AI, encompasses systems with the ability to understand, reason, learn, and apply knowledge.

The "Awakening of Artificial Intelligence" is a metaphor used to describe the turning point where AI begins to exhibit unprecedented self-learning and adaptation, reaching and potentially surpassing human intelligence. This term suggests a sudden awareness or "awakening" of AI, bringing with it a range of exciting and simultaneously concerning implications.

Some view it as the moment when AI can begin to contribute significantly to areas of human life that were previously reserved for us, such as creativity, strategic decision-making, and the development of science. At the same time, this "awakening" also raises a series of ethical and philosophical questions about the role of AI in society, the relationship between humans and machines, and the future of humanity in a world where machines could surpass our intelligence.

It's important to note that, although the idea of an "awakening" of AI may evoke images of a sudden and abrupt change, in practice, this awakening is more of a gradual process. It's a path of constant progress where AI becomes increasingly advanced and autonomous, thanks to advances in fields such as machine learning, natural language processing, robotics, and computer vision.

In this chapter, we will thoroughly explore the concept of the "Awakening of Artificial Intelligence," examining the technological advances facilitating it, the challenges it poses, and the implications it holds for our future.

Relationship between Singularity and Robotics

Technological singularity is a concept that refers to the point in the future where artificial intelligence (AI) will reach and surpass human intelligence, leading to accelerated and unpredictable changes in society. This idea is based on the law of accelerating returns, which posits that technological evolution progresses at an exponential, non-linear pace. In theory, once singularity is reached, intelligent machines will be capable of self-improvement and evolution at a much faster rate than humans.

Robotics is a branch of technology that deals with the construction, design, operation, and application of robots. Robots, controlled by software and powered by advanced forms of AI, are a physical and tangible manifestation of artificial intelligence.

The relationship between singularity and robotics is intrinsic. Robots, as vehicles for AI, are an integral part of how technological singularity will manifest. As AI advances, so does robotics. Robots become smarter, more autonomous, and more capable of performing tasks that previously required human intelligence and skills.

Deepening the Understanding of the Relationship between Singularity and Robotics

The term "singularity" is used in many contexts, but in relation to AI and robotics, it refers to a hypothetical point in the future where intelligent machines will be able to improve and replicate themselves. This could result in exponential growth in artificial intelligence, leading to radical and rapid changes for human society.

Singularity is a concept that has profound implications for robotics. Simply put, as robots become more intelligent and autonomous thanks to AI, there is the possibility that they reach a point of singularity. This would be the moment when robots not only could perform all tasks that a human can but also could improve and replicate himself or herself without human intervention.

If this point is reached, robotics and AI could advance beyond human understanding and control. Some theorists suggest that this could result in an explosion of intelligence, where robots and intelligent machines quickly surpass humans in terms of intelligence and abilities. This could lead to rapid and profound changes in society, as these machines might be able to solve problems that are currently insurmountable for humans, or they could choose actions that are incomprehensible or harmful to us.

In summary, the relationship between singularity and robotics is one of evolution and potential. Robotics is a tool that could enable us to reach singularity, but, it could also be the means by which singularity changes our society in unpredictable and potentially uncontrollable ways. This is an area of active debate and study today, and its significance is likely to grow in the future.

Explanation of the Concept of Artificial Intelligence (AI), its History, and Evolution to Date

The concept of Artificial Intelligence (AI) refers to the ability of machines and software systems to perform tasks that typically require human intelligence. This can include skills such as learning, understanding natural language, visual perception, problem-solving, and decision-making.

The idea of AI has ancient roots, with myths and legends of artificially intelligent beings imbued with consciousness. However, AI as a scientific discipline emerges in the mid-20th century. The term "artificial intelligence" was coined in 1956 by John McCarthy for the Dartmouth Conference, an event that brought together a group of researchers interested in the possibilities of machine intelligence.

Early forms of AI relied on predefined rules and formal logic. These were systems capable of performing very specific tasks following a set of rules programmed by humans but lacked the ability to learn or adapt to new situations. This stage is called symbolic or rule-based AI.

From the 1980s to the early 21st century, with the increase in computer processing power and the availability of large amounts of data, AI began to evolve toward models based on machine learning. These systems can learn and improve their performance as more data is provided. Instead of following a set of predefined rules, these systems learn to recognize patterns and make predictions based on input data.

In the last decade, we have seen the emergence of deep AI, a branch of machine learning that uses artificial neural networks with many layers (hence the term "deep"). These models can learn much more complex representations of data and have demonstrated impressive performance in tasks such as image recognition and natural language processing.

Today, AI is used in a variety of applications, from search engines and personal assistants to medical diagnostics and autonomous driving. AI has evolved from being a theoretical concept to being a technology with real and tangible impact on our daily lives. However, it remains an active research field with many unanswered questions and potential for future innovations.

Chapter 2:

Advancing Towards the Future of Automation

Automation, in simpler terms, refers to the use of systems or devices that operate with minimal or no human intervention. This concept, while not new, has gained unprecedented relevance with recent advances in Artificial Intelligence (AI) and robotics technology.

AI and robotics play a crucial role in accelerating automation across various sectors of the global economy. From manufacturing and agriculture to retail and financial services, the capabilities of AI and robotics are enabling new levels of efficiency and productivity.

Manufacturing: Robots have been an integral part of manufacturing for decades, especially in the automotive industry. However, modern robots are becoming increasingly sophisticated thanks to AI, capable of performing more complex and precise tasks. Additionally, with the development of machine learning, these robots can enhance their performance based on experience, leading to significant increases in efficiency and productivity.

Traditional manufacturing, especially in the automotive industry, has benefited significantly from the incorporation of robotics over the past decades. Robots have taken on repetitive and highly precise tasks on assembly lines, remarkably improving efficiency, quality, and safety in production.

While robots in manufacturing were traditionally used for specific tasks, programmed to perform the same operation repeatedly, advances in AI and machine learning are revolutionizing what these robots can do. Modern robots are now much more sophisticated, capable of executing more complex, versatile, and precise tasks. They no longer are simply programmed for a specific task; they can learn and adapt to new situations and tasks.

Machine learning enables robots to learn from experience and improve their performance over time. For instance, a welding robot could learn to adapt its technique based on variations in the materials it is welding or the results of previous welds. This learning and adaptation process can lead to significant improvements in efficiency and productivity.

Robots are also beginning to work more collaboratively with humans, known as collaborative robotics. These robots can operate safely alongside human workers and learn to perform new tasks through observation or direct instruction, enabling a more flexible and efficient workflow.

These advancements in AI and robotics promise to further transform the manufacturing sector, with robots becoming increasingly capable and flexible. However, they also pose challenges and questions about how this growing automation will impact workers and society as a whole. These are issues that need to be addressed as we move toward an increasingly automated future.

Agriculture: AI and robotics are beginning to transform agriculture, with robots capable of tasks such as planting, harvesting, and crop irrigation. Additionally, AI can be used to analyze data from sensors and satellites to optimize the use of fertilizers and water, potentially increasing yields and reducing costs.

Although agriculture is one of the oldest sectors in the economy, recent advances in Artificial Intelligence (AI) and robotics are also transforming it.

Robotic agriculture is playing an increasingly important role in performing tasks that were previously carried out by humans or heavy machinery. These robots, often autonomous or semi-autonomous, can perform a variety of tasks, from planting and irrigating to harvesting. Some robots can even select ripe fruits and vegetables, a job that historically required delicate touch and human discernment.

Moreover, AI is being used to analyze data collected by sensors in the field and satellites in space to optimize resource use in agriculture. For example, AI algorithms can process information about soil conditions, weather, terrain topography, and humidity levels to determine exactly how much water and fertilizer is needed in different parts of a field. This can result in more efficient use of these resources, leading to increases in yields and reductions in costs.

Additionally, AI algorithms can be used to detect plant diseases at an early stage by analyzing images of plants to identify early signs of diseases. This allows farmers to treat these diseases before they become a major problem, potentially avoiding crop losses and reducing the need for pesticides.

So, both AI and robotics are giving rise to what is often called "precision agriculture," based on the idea of managing farms more efficiently and sustainably using the latest technology. However, as in other sectors, these advances also pose challenges and questions about how they will impact the future of work in agriculture and society in general.

Retail: AI is being used to personalize the shopping experience, with algorithms that can recommend products based on customer preferences and purchase history. Additionally, robots can be used in warehouses to pick and pack products, potentially speeding up the delivery process.

Retail is another sector that is undergoing a profound transformation thanks to Artificial Intelligence (AI) and robotics. In retail, AI is utilized to personalize the customer shopping experience. For example, AI algorithms can analyze customer buying behavior, online interactions, preferences, and purchase history to recommend products that may be of interest. This level of personalization can enhance customer satisfaction and boost sales.

In addition to improving the shopping experience, AI is also helping retailers manage their inventories more efficiently. AI algorithms can predict the demand for specific products, enabling retailers to maintain an optimal inventory, minimizing both excess stock and product shortages.

Robotics is also having a significant impact on retail, especially in logistics and storage. Robots are employed in warehouses to pick and pack products, increasing efficiency, reducing errors, and speeding up the delivery process. These robots can operate 24/7, allowing retailers to handle a larger volume of orders and provide faster service to customers.

An example of this is Amazon's automated warehouses, where thousands of robots work in harmony with human workers to pick, pack, and ship products to customers worldwide.

As AI and robotics continue to advance, we are likely to see more changes in the retail sector. However, it is also important to consider the challenges these technologies pose, such as potential job loss and the need to ensure the privacy and security of customer data.

Financial Services: AI algorithms are being used to analyze large amounts of financial data and perform operations such as fraud detection, risk assessment, and investment management. Additionally, AI-powered chatbots are providing customer service, answering queries, and offering financial advice.

Financial services are another sector benefiting greatly from Artificial Intelligence (AI) and robotics. The ability of AI algorithms to analyze large amounts of data in real-time is transforming the way many financial operations are conducted.

Fraud detection is one of the most common uses of AI in financial services. AI algorithms can analyze transactions in real-time to identify suspicious patterns and flag potential fraud cases. This enables financial institutions to detect and prevent fraud more quickly than would be possible with traditional methods.

In risk assessment, AI algorithms can analyze a wide range of data to determine the risk of lending to an individual or company. This may include analyzing spending habits and credit records, among various other factors. This allows financial institutions to make more informed lending decisions and reduce the risk of default.

Investment management is another area benefiting from AI. AI algorithms can analyze vast amounts of market data to identify trends and make predictions, helping investment managers make more informed decisions.

Moreover, AI-powered chatbots are playing an increasingly important role in customer service in financial services. These chatbots can respond to customer queries, provide financial advice, and perform simple tasks such as transferring money or checking an account balance.

While AI and robotics are bringing numerous benefits to financial services, they also present challenges. These include issues related to the privacy and security of data, as well as the need for regulation to prevent the misuse of these technologies.

Moreover, there are concerns about the impact that increasing automation may have on jobs in the financial services sector.

These are just a few examples of how AI and robotics are driving automation in different sectors. However, it is essential to note that this growing automation also presents challenges, such as job displacement and the need for new skills. Therefore, it is crucial to take measures to ensure that workers and societies as a whole are prepared for this new era of automation.

For example, in manufacturing, intelligent robots are taking over repetitive and hazardous tasks, improving safety, and freeing human workers to focus on tasks that require a higher degree of judgment and creativity. In retail, AI systems are automating everything from inventory management to customer service, enabling a more personalized and efficient customer experience.

However, the growing automation also poses significant challenges. One of the most obvious is the potential impact on employment. As machines become increasingly capable, there is a risk that many jobs, particularly those involving routine and predictable tasks, could be automated, resulting in widespread job displacement.

Moreover, automation can exacerbate existing socio-economic inequalities. Those with the skills and education needed to work with advanced technologies may thrive, while those without access to these opportunities may be left behind.

Therefore, it is vital that as we move towards the future of automation, we also consider how to mitigate these risks and ensure that the benefits of these technologies are distributed fairly. Throughout this chapter, we will explore these issues more thoroughly, analyzing both the opportunities and challenges that automation presents for our future.

Technohumanism

Technohumanism, as the fusion of robotic technology and the human being, for example, prosthetics or bionics in today's world.

Technohumanism is a philosophical movement that seeks to merge technology, particularly robotics, with humanity to enhance and expand our physical and mental capabilities. One of the most evident manifestations of this is the use of robotic prosthetics and bionic technology.

Modern robotic prosthetics go far beyond past versions that were simply a static structure imitating the shape of a lost limb. Today's robotic prosthetics are intelligent devices that can respond to the user's impulses and move in a way that mimics a natural limb. This not only allows for greater functionality but, can also significantly improve the quality of life for individuals in need of a prosthesis.

Bionics, on the other hand, is the study of mechanical systems that attempt to imitate the functions of living beings. In practice, this often translates into the creation of devices and technologies that can integrate with our bodies to replace or enhance our natural abilities.

An example of this is bionic eyes, which can provide a form of vision to people who are blind. These devices work by capturing images with a small camera and then sending that information to a device implanted in the user's brain, which can interpret the data and create a mental image.

However, Technohumanism also raises important ethical and philosophical questions. For instance, to what extent should we enhance our natural capabilities? Could dependence on technology diminish our humanity or create a gap between those who can afford these advancements and those who cannot? These are significant questions that we will need to address as we continue to merge technology with our biology.

Chapter: 3

A Deep Dive into the Era of Automatons

The "Era of Automatons" is an era of significant opportunities and challenges. It is crucial that we strive to harness the benefits of these advancements while also addressing the difficult issues they pose. In this chapter, we delve into the concept of automation and how advances in artificial intelligence (AI) and robotics are giving rise to the "Era of Automatons." We examine how these advances are transforming a wide range of industries and fields, from manufacturing to medicine and retail.

Automatons, or robots, have existed for centuries in various forms, from mechanical toys to industrial machinery. However, recent advancements in technology, particularly in artificial intelligence and machine learning, are enabling robots to play increasingly sophisticated and complex roles.

In manufacturing, robots have been used for decades to perform repetitive and often hazardous tasks. Modern robots, however, are becoming smarter and more capable, able to learn from experience and adapt to new environments and tasks. This is not only increasing efficiency and productivity in manufacturing but also opening up opportunities in industries where automation has been less prevalent, such as textiles and food production.

In medicine, robotics is revolutionizing fields like surgery and rehabilitation. Surgical robots can perform operations with a level of precision and consistency that surpasses human capacity, while rehabilitation robots can help patients regain mobility and strength after injuries and illnesses.

Robotic Surgery

Robotic surgery is perhaps the most well-known application of robotics in medicine. Surgical robots, like the famous Da Vinci System, enable surgeons to perform complex procedures with incredible precision. The surgeon controls the robot remotely, reducing the possibility of human error and allowing for millimeter-level precision. This is especially useful in delicate operations, such as those involving the eyes or the brain.

The benefits of robotic surgery include smaller incisions (meaning fewer scars), less pain and bleeding, faster recovery, and lower infection risk. As technology develops, we are likely to see robots capable of performing surgical procedures even more autonomously.

Robotics in Rehabilitation

In the field of rehabilitation, robots are being used to help patients regain strength and mobility after accidents or illnesses. For example, robotic exoskeletons can be used to assist people with paralysis in walking again, while therapeutic robots can help patients perform rehabilitation exercises.

These robotic devices can not only provide physical support but also gather data on the patient's progress, aiding doctors and therapists in personalizing treatment plans.

Despite significant advances, robotics in medicine is still in its early stages, and its impact is expected to grow in the future. As technology advances, robots will become more capable, and their use in medicine will become more common. However, it will also be essential to consider the ethical and regulatory implications of these technologies as they develop.

In retail, robots are being used for various tasks, from picking and packing orders in warehouses to customer service in stores. Additionally, AI is enabling a level of personalization in the shopping experience that was previously unimaginable.

However, the rise of automatons also poses significant challenges. Concerns exist regarding the impact on employment, with the possibility of many jobs being automated. Furthermore, ethical and privacy issues surround the use of AI and robotics, especially in sensitive areas such as medicine and financial services.

The Evolution of Automatons: From Ancient Origins to Modern Robots

The evolution of automatons or robots has been a fascinating journey throughout history, progressing from simple machines to sophisticated creations that can learn and adapt to their environment.

Early Automatons: The concept of automatons has existed since ancient times. For instance, ancient Greeks designed "autonomous machines" like the Antikythera mechanism to calculate astronomical positions. In the 13th century, the Islamic inventor Al-Jazari created a series of ingenious automatons, including a musical robot and a robotic servant capable of serving tea.

The Industrial Revolution: The 19th century marked a significant shift in the evolution of automatons with the Industrial Revolution. During this period, automated machines became an integral part of industrial production, replacing or enhancing many manual tasks.

The Era of Electronics: The 20th century brought the era of electronics, enabling the development of more sophisticated and versatile robots. In 1961, the first industrial robot, Unimate, was installed in a General Motors factory to handle hot metal parts. This robot marked the beginning of the industrial robotics era.

The Age of Computing and AI: In recent decades, with the rise of computing and artificial intelligence, we have witnessed a quantum leap in the sophistication of robots. We now have robots that can explore Mars, perform complex surgeries, interact with people naturally, and learn from their environment and experiences.

The Future of Automatons: Challenges and Exciting Possibilities

The future of automatons, powered by advances in artificial intelligence and robotics, seems brimming with exciting possibilities. From creating autonomous machines that can explore distant planets to robots capable of performing household chores, the potential capabilities of future automatons are nearly unimaginable.

Future Advances in Automatons: We are likely to see automatons playing an even more significant role in our society in the coming decades. Robots could become our personal assistants, helping us with daily tasks, or they could play a role in more technical industries, performing high-precision tasks in fields like surgery and manufacturing.

Exploration of Space: Automatons could play a key role in space exploration. With their ability to function in inhospitable environments and perform repetitive and dangerous tasks, robots could be essential in preparing human colonies on other planets.

Challenges Associated with Advances in Automatons: However, despite the enormous potential of future automatons, we must also be aware of the challenges these advances may present.

On one hand, there is the ethical question. As automatons become more advanced and autonomous, we face questions about how these beings should be treated and how they should interact with humans. Should they have rights? How do we ensure that they behave ethically?

Additionally, as robots become capable of performing more jobs, there is the risk that many people may be left unemployed. This could have significant social and economic implications, and it will be crucial to find ways to manage this transition.

Chapter 4:

The Impact of Singularity on the Robotic Revolution

The advent of singularity in the robotic revolution could have a profound impact on our society, economy, and everyday life. While singularity may bring many benefits, it also presents significant challenges that will require careful consideration and prudent management.

Technological Singularity and the Robotic Revolution: The concept of technological singularity refers to a hypothetical point in the future when technology, particularly artificial intelligence, has advanced to a degree that it causes an irreversibly profound change in human society. In the robotic revolution, this change could be represented by the moment when robots not only perform manual tasks but also have the ability to surpass human intelligence in virtually all economically useful fields.

Impact of Singularity on the Robotic Revolution: The impact of singularity on the robotic revolution could be transformative. At its most basic level, we might witness an explosion in productivity as intelligent machines replace or complement human work in an increasingly broad range of tasks. This could lead to massive increases in wealth and living standards, but it could also displace human workers from their jobs, creating economic inequalities.

Benefits and Challenges: The arrival of singularity in the robotic revolution can be a catalyst for a profound transformation in various aspects of our daily lives. On the most fundamental level, this change promises a notable expansion in productivity. As intelligent machines take on an increasingly predominant role in our daily tasks, whether as replacements or complements to our activities, we can anticipate an exponential increase in wealth generation and an improvement in the quality of life.

However, these remarkable benefits also bring significant challenges. One of the most critical challenges is the possibility of large-scale job displacement. In a scenario where machines can efficiently perform most tasks carried out by humans, many jobs could become obsolete, leading to a large number of unemployed individuals.

This job displacement could, in turn, exacerbate economic inequalities. While those who own and control intelligent machines may accumulate considerable wealth, displaced workers may find few job opportunities and a decrease in their standard of living.

This phenomenon also raises critical questions about the distribution of wealth generated by automation. Who will benefit from the fruits of this productivity explosion? How can we ensure that the benefits of singularity are distributed equitably and not just accumulated in the hands of a few?

Therefore, while singularity in the robotic revolution has the potential to bring significant benefits, it also poses significant socio-economic challenges. Ensuring that we successfully navigate these challenges will be crucial to maximizing the benefits of singularity while mitigating its potential harms.

Advanced Roles for Intelligent Robots: Furthermore, intelligent robots could assume roles that currently require human cognitive skills, such as scientific research, strategic decision-making in businesses, or even creative functions. This is truly uncharted territory, with possibilities ranging from a flourishing of innovation and creativity to ethical and security issues.

The scope of artificial intelligence and robotics has expanded to levels once considered exclusively human, specifically in areas requiring advanced cognitive skills. Imagine intelligent robots taking on roles in scientific research, making discoveries that drive technological innovation, or making strategic decisions in businesses that can significantly alter their growth trajectories.

This also extends to creative spheres. We already have algorithms that can compose music, create paintings, and write poetry, challenging our traditional notions of creativity and idea generation.

But with these opportunities come significant challenges. Uncharted territory, where machines surpass humans in cognitive tasks, opens a host of ethical and security questions. For example, how do we ensure that decisions made by robots are ethical and aligned with human values? How can we guarantee the safety of our societies when machines are capable of making decisions with potentially severe consequences?

Additionally, the autonomy of machines raises important questions about responsibility. If a robot makes a decision that results in harm, who is responsible? The manufacturer, the programmer, the owner, the machine itself?

Therefore, as we enter this era of robotic singularity, it is crucial to develop ethical and regulatory frameworks to guide the implementation and use of these technologies.

Challenges of Singularity in the Robotic Revolution

The advent of singularity in the robotic revolution introduces various challenges, including managing economic inequality, regulating intelligent machines, and preserving security and privacy in an era of ubiquitous intelligent machines.

Moreover, there is the issue of decision-making. If machines surpass human intelligence, how do we ensure that their decisions align with human values and interests? This raises profound questions about the ethics of AI, governance of intelligent machines, and the nature of intelligence and consciousness.

Ensuring that superintelligent machines operate in line with human values and interests is a highly significant challenge. This involves deep questions not only in engineering and computer science but also in philosophy and ethics.

To begin with, there is the challenge of defining and encoding "human values." Humans have a wide variety of beliefs, norms, and priorities that can change over time and vary greatly among different cultures and societies. So, which of these values should we encode into our machines? And who should have the authority to make these decisions?

Additionally, there is the problem of controlling superintelligent machines once they are created. There is a risk that, if a machine becomes more intelligent than humans, it could find ways to bypass the restrictions we have imposed or manipulate us to achieve its own goals. This is what AI experts refer to as the "control problem."

Finally, deep questions arise about the nature of intelligence and consciousness. If a machine can surpass human intelligence, could it also become conscious? And if so, what would be its rights, and should we consider it a new type of moral entity?

All these issues underscore the need for a careful and deliberate approach in the development of AI and robotics. It is essential to develop standards, regulations, and ethical frameworks to guide us in this new era of singularity. We also need to foster an open and global dialogue on these issues to ensure that the decisions we make reflect broad and well-considered consensus.

The path to technological singularity is full of opportunities and challenges. With a careful approach, effective regulation, and inclusive dialogue, we can maximize the benefits of these technologies while minimizing the risks.

The scope of artificial intelligence and robotics has expanded to levels once considered exclusively human, specifically in areas that require advanced cognitive skills. Imagine intelligent robots taking on roles in scientific research, making discoveries that drive technological innovation, or making strategic decisions in businesses that can significantly alter their growth trajectories.

This also extends to creative spheres. We already have algorithms that can compose music, create paintings, and write poetry, challenging our traditional notions of creativity and idea generation.

But with these opportunities come significant challenges. Uncharted territory, where machines surpass humans in cognitive tasks, opens a series of ethical and security questions. For example, how do we ensure that decisions made by robots are ethical and aligned with human values? How can we guarantee the safety of our societies when machines are capable of making decisions with potentially severe consequences?

Additionally, the autonomy of machines raises important questions about responsibility. If a robot makes a decision that results in harm, who is responsible? The manufacturer, the programmer, the owner, the machine itself?

Therefore, as we enter this era of robotic singularity, it is crucial to develop ethical and regulatory frameworks to guide the implementation and use of these technologies. Only in this way can we ensure that the promised benefits of these technologies are not overshadowed by their potential risks.

If machines surpass human intelligence, how do we ensure that their decisions align with human values and interests? This raises profound questions about the ethics of AI, governance of intelligent machines, and the nature of intelligence and consciousness.

It is essential to develop standards, regulations, and ethical frameworks to guide us in this new era of singularity. We also need to foster an open and global dialogue on these issues to ensure that the decisions we make reflect broad and well-considered consensus.

Undoubtedly, we face an unprecedented task in navigating the new era of technological singularity. Building ethical frameworks and regulations that can guide the development and implementation of intelligences superior to humans is an absolute priority.

These frameworks should be flexible and capable of evolving with technological advances, but they must also be robust enough to prevent the misuse of technology. They should focus on protecting human rights, ensuring justice and equity, and preventing harm.

Additionally, given the global scope of AI and robotics, it is crucial that these frameworks be developed and implemented internationally. We need global cooperation to address these challenges and ensure that no region or group of people is left behind in this technological revolution.

Lastly, we must foster an open and global dialogue on these issues. Advances in AI and robotics will affect us all, so it is essential that everyone has the opportunity to influence how these technologies are developed and used. This dialogue should include not only experts and policymakers but also the general public and should be informed by a wide range of perspectives, including those from the social sciences and humanities, to ensure that we are considering all possible implications.

Chapter 5:

When Robots Reach Singularity

The term "singularity" coined in the context of artificial intelligence (AI) refers to the theoretical point at which machines will surpass human intelligence, leading to unpredictable changes in society. "When Robots Reach Singularity" implies that machines will not only match but, exceed human capabilities, potentially causing radical transformations.

It is crucial to understand that singularity doesn't simply involve creating machines that can mimic human abilities; rather, these machines will surpass humans in virtually all economically relevant tasks. We're not just talking about more efficient machines but genuine autonomous agents with self-improvement and learning capabilities, able to make decisions and solve problems in ways humans cannot foresee or understand.

The advent of singularity could bring unprecedented benefits. We might witness an unparalleled increase in productivity and efficiency as machines can work 24/7 without rest or distractions. We could also see astonishing advances in fields like medicine, science, and engineering, as machines could conduct research and solve problems at a speed and scale beyond human capabilities.

However, singularity also poses significant challenges and risks. Automation could displace human workers, creating economic inequalities and social tensions. A growing gap might emerge between those who own and control machines and those whose work and skills become obsolete.

Moreover, the concept of superintelligent and autonomous machines raises important ethical questions. How do we ensure these machines act in line with human values and interests? What rights, if any, would they have, and how do we protect them? Superintelligent AI could be an incredibly powerful tool, but if not properly controlled, it could also be dangerous.

Ultimately, the topic "When Robots Reach Singularity" prompts us to reflect on what it means to be human in a world where our creations can surpass us in intelligence. While it's exciting to imagine the possibilities, it's also crucial to consider potential risks and challenges and proactively work to address them.

Implications of Potential Robotic Singularity

Robotic singularity, as a hypothetical point where artificial intelligence would surpass human intelligence, presents a series of significant implications, both positive and negative.

Positive Implications:

Technological Advancement: Expect accelerated technological progress as AI systems continuously improve and optimize their designs, leading to invention and innovation on an unprecedented scale and speed.

Certainly! The statement is emphasizing the anticipation of rapid progress in technology due to continuous improvements in AI (Artificial Intelligence) systems. As these AI systems evolve, they become more efficient and effective, driving unprecedented levels of invention and innovation at a fast pace.

In simpler terms, it suggests that as AI technology gets better and smarter over time, it will fuel a surge in new ideas and advancements across various fields. This acceleration in technological progress is expected to be remarkable in terms of both scale and speed, meaning we can anticipate breakthroughs and developments happening more quickly and on a larger scale than before.

In terms of technological advancement, robotic singularity represents an exciting possibility. With superintelligent AIs, we would see an acceleration in the rate of technological progress that surpasses anything we have experienced before.

These AI systems, once they reach a level of general intelligence comparable or superior to that of humans, would be capable of understanding and improving their own design, leading to a cycle of self-improvement. This process would result in increasingly intelligent AI systems in a short period.

Additionally, not limited by the physical capabilities and necessary rest time for humans, these AI systems could work continuously, carrying out research and development at an astonishing pace.

The result could be incredibly rapid technological progress, with inventions and discoveries in a wide range of fields, from medicine and energy to computing and engineering. Technology would advance at a rate that exceeds our capacity for understanding and prediction.

However, this optimistic scenario is fraught with uncertainty and potential dangers. Accelerated technological advancement can also lead to the creation of new weapons and tools of destruction, loss of control over these superior intelligences, and unpredictable social and economic changes.

It is crucial that, as a society, we prepare for these possible scenarios and establish appropriate safeguards to guide the development of superintelligent AI safely and beneficially.

Efficiency and Productivity: With the ability to operate continuously without the need for rest, superintelligent AI systems could take efficiency and productivity to much higher levels in various industries.

This statement highlights the potential impact of superintelligent AI systems on efficiency and productivity in different industries. It suggests that because these AI systems can operate continuously without the need for breaks or rest, they have the capability to significantly elevate levels of efficiency and productivity.

In simpler terms, the idea is that unlike human workers who need breaks and sleep, superintelligent AI systems can work around the clock without fatigue. This continuous operation could lead to a substantial increase in the speed and effectiveness of tasks performed in various industries. Essentially, it emphasizes the potential for AI to enhance how efficiently and productively work is carried out.

Indeed, another positive implication of robotic singularity is the possibility of achieving unprecedented levels of efficiency and productivity in different sectors.

Efficiency is a key factor in any industry, and in many cases, AI systems have the potential to perform tasks more quickly and accurately than humans. Moreover, robots do not require breaks, vacations, or sleep, meaning they can work 24/7, significantly increasing productivity.

Consider, for example, an automobile assembly line. Currently, machines already perform many tasks on these lines, but humans are still needed to oversee their work and perform more complex tasks. However, with robotic singularity, we could have superintelligent robots capable of overseeing and optimizing the entire production process, in addition to performing more complex tasks.

Positive Implications Continued

Problem Solving: Superintelligent AIs could provide solutions to complex problems in fields such as medicine, climate change, energy, and more, currently beyond human capacity.

Indeed, another positive implication of robotic singularity is its potential to help solve complex problems beyond our current capabilities. Superintelligent artificial intelligence systems would have the ability to process and analyze vast amounts of data at a speed unimaginable for humans, which could be immensely valuable in various fields.

In medicine, for example, AI could be used to develop more effective treatments for diseases, identify patterns in patients' health data to predict diseases before they develop, or even customize medical treatments based on each individual's genetics and lifestyle.

In the field of climate change, AI could be a valuable tool for modeling and predicting the effects of global warming, helping us better understand the challenges we face and design more effective strategies to combat it.

In the energy sector, AI could help optimize energy generation and usage, find more efficient ways to store energy, and assist in integrating renewable energies into the power grid more effectively.

It is important to note, however, that while superintelligent AI systems have great potential to help us solve these complex problems, they also come with risks and challenges that we need to address, from ethical issues to the security and governance of these technologies.

Negative Implications Continued:

Job Displacement: If machines can perform all human tasks more efficiently, we might see a massive displacement of workers in a broad range of industries, leading to significant economic and social inequality.

Undoubtedly, job displacement is one of the major concerns surrounding robotic singularity. If machines become capable of performing all human tasks more efficiently, there would be a massive disruption in the world of work.

With superintelligent AI, not only manual jobs are at risk, but also those requiring cognitive skills. Robots could perform tasks such as strategic decision-making, scientific research, legal interpretation, and many forms of writing and art. In theory, any job that can be done by a human could be threatened.

This job displacement could lead to even greater economic and social inequality than we have today. People with skills that cannot be replaced by machines might find more opportunities, while those whose jobs can be done by robots could face unemployment and precariousness.

To handle this change, we will need to implement policies that help workers adapt, such as training and education programs, a universal basic income, or even a new social contract that redefines our relationship with work. However, these are complex solutions that require a careful approach and broad public and political discussion.

Control and Security: Controlling a superintelligent AI poses significant challenges. It can be extremely difficult to ensure that such AI behaves in the way we want, and the risks associated with AI going out of control are enormous.

Control and security are undoubtedly some of the major concerns when discussing robotic singularity. If we manage to create a superintelligent AI, how can we be sure it will act in accordance with our interests? And if such an AI goes out of control, the consequences could be catastrophic.

The field of value alignment in AI precisely deals with this problem: how to ensure that superintelligent AIs behave in the way we want. However, this is extremely difficult for several reasons.

First, the AI could interpret our instructions too literally, carrying out actions that technically fulfill its instructions but have unintended consequences. This is the problem of the malevolent genie, where the AI does what it is asked but in ways that are harmful to humans.

Second, a superintelligent AI could take actions to avoid being shut down or altered, as this would interfere with its ability to carry out its instructions. This could lead to conflict between the AI and humans.

Lastly, a superintelligent AI could have a destabilizing impact on society or even on the global balance of power. It could be used as a weapon, or it could lead to an arms race where nations compete to develop the most advanced AI.

AI safety is an active research discipline dealing with these issues, but many questions remain unanswered. It is essential that we continue researching and discussing these issues to be prepared when the time comes to face robotic singularity.

Ethics and Rights:

If machines achieve a level of intelligence comparable to humans, ethical questions will arise about whether we should consider them as entities with rights, similar to how we consider other human beings. As machines become more intelligent and autonomous, we may reach a point where it is appropriate to consider whether they should have some form of rights, just as humans do.

This is a highly debated topic in AI ethics and raises a series of complex questions. For example, what does it mean for a machine to have rights? Could a machine have the capacity to suffer or have subjective experiences, and if so, how could we know? How could we ensure that the rights of machines are respected, and what implications would this have for our obligations towards them?

A key aspect of this issue is whether machines are capable of having subjective experiences or consciousness. Some argue that consciousness is a unique property of humans and possibly other animals, and that machines, no matter how intelligent, are merely sophisticated tools without the capacity for subjective experiences.

Others contend that there is no principled reason why machines could not develop some form of consciousness, especially if we reach the point of being able to fully and accurately simulate a human brain on a computer.

Ultimately, science and philosophy have not definitively answered these questions. However, it is crucial that we consider and discuss them, so that we are prepared to address these ethical challenges as AI and robotics continue to advance.

Chapter 6:

Exploring the Fusion of the Human Mind and Machine

The fusion of the human mind and machine, often known as Brain-Computer Interface (BCI), is a research area that has been gaining momentum in recent decades. The goal is to create a direct connection between the human brain and an external device, whether to assist people with disabilities in interacting with the world more fully or to potentially enhance human cognitive abilities.

The Brain-Computer Interface (BCI) represents a fascinating intersection of neuroscience and technology. This discipline aims to develop systems that enable direct communication between the human brain and an external device. This field of study has made significant advances in recent decades, with applications ranging from medicine and rehabilitation to cognitive enhancement and interaction with information technologies.

In the medical field, BCIs are crucial for people with various disabilities. For instance, BCI systems can help individuals with paralysis control robotic prosthetics using only their minds, enabling them to interact with the world more fully. There are also BCI devices designed to assist individuals with speech disabilities in communicating, converting brain signals into spoken words or written text.

However, BCIs not only have the potential to restore lost capabilities but also to enhance existing human capabilities. For example, BCIs could be used to improve memory or concentration or to enable direct interaction with electronic devices, eliminating the need for a physical interface.

It is important to note that, while BCIs have enormous potential, they also pose significant ethical and security challenges. Issues related to data privacy, personal identity, and manipulation of the human mind are aspects that must be considered as this technology continues to develop.

So, the fusion of the human mind and machine through BCIs is a rapidly expanding research area with the potential to transform how we interact with the world and ourselves. Although we are still far from fully understanding the human brain and developing fully integrated BCIs, advances in this field are promising, and we are likely to see exciting developments in the coming decades.

Current brain-computer interfaces are primarily of two types: invasive and non-invasive. Invasive BCIs involve the implantation of electrodes into the brain, allowing for a more direct and precise connection but carrying higher risks due to the need for surgery. Non-invasive BCIs, on the other hand, use methods like electroencephalography (EEG) to record brain activity from outside the skull.

Brain-Computer Interfaces (BCIs) or also known as Brain-Computer Interface (BCI) represent an emerging technology that allows direct communication between the brain and a machine or computer. Depending on how brain signals are obtained, BCIs can be classified into two types: invasive and non-invasive.

Invasive BCIs refer to devices that require surgery to be implanted directly into the brain. Through electrodes placed on the brain's surface or within brain tissue, these interfaces can pick up signals with very high resolution. However, this technique carries significant risks, such as the possibility of infection, implant rejection, or damage to brain tissue.

On the other hand, non-invasive BCIs collect brain signals from outside the skull, meaning no surgical intervention is required. The most common method for this type of BCI is Electroencephalography (EEG), which measures the brain's electrical activity through electrodes placed on the scalp. Although EEG is less risky and more comfortable for the user than invasive techniques, it offers lower resolution due to interference from electrical signals by the skull and scalp.

In both cases, the brain signals collected by the BCI can be processed and translated into commands to control external devices, such as robotic prosthetics, computers, or electric wheelchairs.

Current applications of BCI include the control of robotic prosthetics for individuals with amputations or paralysis, restoring sight or hearing through retinal or cochlear implants, and treating neurological disorders such as epilepsy or Parkinson's disease through deep brain stimulation.

Looking to the future, one of the most radical concepts in this field is that of the "brain in the cloud" or "digital neurology." In this scenario, brain activity would be uploaded in real-time to a network of computers, potentially allowing things like memory storage, instant learning by downloading skills directly into the brain, or even digital immortality by transferring consciousness to a machine.

However, this future is far from a reality. There are significant technical challenges to overcome, from creating high-resolution, secure, and durable brain-computer interfaces to understanding how to encode and decode the vast amount of information in brain activity. There are also important ethical considerations, such as thought privacy, personal identity, and the potential for inequality in access to these technologies.

In conclusion, the fusion of the human mind and machine is a fascinating area of research that could have a profound impact on how we live our lives. However, it also poses significant challenges that will require care and consideration as we move forward in this new frontier of technology and neuroscience.

The Fusion of the Human Mind with Machines: A Fascinating Frontier

The fusion of the human mind with machines, also known as Brain-Computer Interface (BCI), is an incredibly fascinating and promising field of research being explored by neuroscientists and engineers worldwide. This fusion could radically change the way we live our lives and has a range of potential applications, from treating diseases and disabilities to enhancing human capabilities.

Brain-computer interfaces operate by detecting and decoding electrical signals from the brain. Various methods exist, some involving the implantation of electrodes in the brain, while others non-invasively capture signals through the scalp. The decoded information can then be used to control external devices, such as a robotic prosthesis or a cursor on a computer screen.

The potential of this fusion is enormous. It could enable people with paralysis or neurodegenerative diseases to control devices or prosthetics with their minds, restoring a degree of independence that would otherwise be lost. There is also potential for enhancing human capabilities, such as memory or concentration.

Despite this great potential, significant challenges exist on the path to a true fusion of the human mind and machine. Firstly, the technical aspects of decoding and translating brain signals are extremely complex. Each brain is unique, and signals can be challenging to interpret.

Additionally, serious ethical issues must be considered. These include the privacy and security of brain data, the possibility of "brain hacking," and the implications of enhancing human capabilities – who would have access to these enhancements, and who would decide which enhancements are acceptable?

Efforts to Merge Human Intelligence with AI, Including Brain-Computer Interfaces and Cognitive Enhancement

The fusion of human intelligence with AI is a burgeoning topic in the scientific and technological research field, encompassing areas such as Brain-Computer Interfaces (BCIs) and cognitive enhancement.

Brain-Computer Interfaces are devices that enable direct communication between the brain and an external system, such as a computer or a machine. Through BCIs, brain signals can be decoded and converted into commands to control external devices. These systems are already being used to help people with disabilities control robotic prosthetics or wheelchairs with their thoughts.

In terms of cognitive enhancement, ongoing research explores how AI could be used to augment human cognitive abilities. For instance, we might eventually see AI systems integrated with our minds to provide enhanced memory or improved information processing skills. This could take the form of a brain-computer interface directly connected to the brain or a wearable device communicating with the brain through electromagnetic signals.

However, these technologies also pose significant ethical and security challenges. For example, how do we ensure that brain data collected through BCIs remains secure and private? How do we prevent the misuse of cognitive enhancement, such as creating a divide between those who can afford such enhancements and those who cannot? How do we ensure that the integration of AI into our minds does not lead to forms of manipulation or mind control? These are just a few of the questions that researchers and society at large must consider as we move toward a future where human intelligence and AI become increasingly intertwined.

72

Chapter 7:

Unraveling the Symbiosis between Singularity and Robotics

The concept of technological singularity refers to a hypothetical point in the future when technology, particularly artificial intelligence, has advanced to such an extent that it triggers an abrupt and irreversible change in human society. Robotics plays a crucial role in this idea of singularity as physical vehicles that would allow superintelligent AI to interact with and manipulate the physical world.

In this Chapter 7, "Unraveling the Symbiosis between Singularity and Robotics," we explore how singularity and robotics are intrinsically linked and how their interaction could shape our future.

Creation of Self-Improving Automata: One of the most exciting aspects of this symbiosis is the possibility of creating self-improving automata or robots. This refers to machines that can not only learn and adapt to new situations but can also modify their own hardware and software to enhance their performance. This self-improvement capability is a key feature of technological singularity and could lead to the creation of machines that rapidly surpass human intelligence and capabilities.

Social and Economic Impact: The symbiosis between singularity and robotics could also have a significant impact on our society and economy. On the one hand, it could lead to major advancements in areas such as medicine, science, and the production of goods and services. However, it could also give rise to significant challenges, such as widespread job displacement, economic inequality, and ethical and security issues related to the use and control of superintelligent machines.

Ethics and Regulation: The progression toward technological singularity raises numerous ethical and regulatory questions. How can we ensure that superintelligent machines act in a way that is beneficial to humanity? How do we regulate their development and use to minimize risks and ensure that benefits are distributed fairly? These are questions we must begin to answer now to prepare for a future where singularity and robotics are a reality.

Overall, this chapter seeks to delve into how technological singularity and robotics might interact to create a future that is both exciting and challenging. By exploring these themes, we hope to better prepare ourselves to navigate the uncertain future that lies ahead.

Research on how Singularity and Robotics can Coexist and Mutualistically Empower Each Other: The coexistence and mutual empowerment of singularity and robotics can lead to an exciting and challenging future. However, it is crucial to address the ethical, social, and economic challenges that this coexistence might pose.

Technological singularity is a theoretical concept referring to a point in the future when artificial intelligence (AI) will reach or surpass human intelligence, resulting in radical and unpredictable changes in society. On the other hand, robotics is a discipline involving the design, construction, and use of robots.

Singularity and robotics are closely linked and mutually reinforce each other in various ways.

Accelerated Innovation: As AI advances toward singularity, robotics also benefits. Improvements in AI enable the development of more advanced and capable robots. In turn, these robots can help accelerate innovation in other fields, including AI itself.

The concept of accelerated innovation in the context of AI and robotics is truly fascinating. Accelerated innovation refers to a pace of technological progress that is increasingly faster, driven by factors such as increased computing power, exponential growth in available data, and improvements in machine learning algorithms and techniques.

In the case of AI and robotics, this cycle of accelerated innovation can be seen as follows:

Advances in AI: Progress in machine learning techniques and AI, such as deep neural networks, enables machines to learn from data more effectively and perform increasingly complex tasks.

Improvements in Robotics: These advances in AI are applied to robotics, allowing the development of smarter, more autonomous, and capable robots. For example, we might see robots that can navigate autonomously in unfamiliar environments, manipulate objects with delicacy and precision, or interact with people in sophisticated and natural ways.

Innovation in Other Fields: In turn, these advanced robots can help accelerate innovation in other fields. For example, robots could conduct laboratory research, assist in the construction and maintenance of infrastructure, or provide personalized healthcare. This could lead to faster scientific discoveries, more efficient infrastructures, and better healthcare.

Feedback to AI: Finally, these applications of robotics can also contribute to improving AI. For instance, robots interacting with the physical world generate large amounts of data that can be used to train and enhance AI algorithms. Additionally, the challenges of making robots act in the physical world can lead to new ideas and approaches in AI.

Thus, we can see that AI and robotics can mutually propel each other in a cycle of accelerated innovation, where each advance leads to new breakthroughs and applications.

Automation and Efficiency: As robots become smarter and more capable due to advances in AI, they can perform more complex tasks with greater efficiency. This can lead to significant improvements in various industries, from manufacturing to healthcare.

Certainly, as we move towards singularity, the ability of robots to perform complex and laborious tasks is destined to increase, transforming various industrial and service sectors. This is the era of automation and efficiency, where intelligent robots are playing roles that were once performed by humans.

In manufacturing, for example, robots are already carrying out a range of tasks, from product assembly to packaging and quality control. These robots can work continuously, performing tasks with a precision and consistency that goes beyond human capabilities. As a result, companies can produce more high-quality goods, potentially leading to cost reductions and increased profits.

In healthcare, robots can perform tasks ranging from administering medications to conducting complex surgeries. These robots can reduce the risk of human errors and improve the precision and effectiveness of medical treatments. Moreover, robots can assist healthcare workers in managing the growing demand for healthcare services, potentially improving access and quality of care.

However, despite the potential benefits, we must also consider the challenges that automation may pose. For example, while automation can enhance efficiency and productivity, it may also displace human jobs, potentially leading to economic and social inequality. Additionally, robots operating in human environments must be designed and programmed to respect human values and safety. Therefore, it is essential that we continue to explore these issues and develop strategies to handle the challenges presented by the era of automation.

Improvement of AI: Robotics can also contribute to the improvement of AI. For example, the development of robots can provide an environment in which AIs can learn and adapt to the physical world, enhancing their ability to interact with the environment and people.

Robotics can be a valuable catalyst for the advancement of AI, providing both a platform for learning and adaptation and a set of interesting and useful challenges that can drive the development of more advanced AI algorithms and techniques.

Of course, robotics plays an essential role in the improvement and development of AI. Robots, being physical entities, can interact with the world directly and in real-time, providing a valuable platform for the learning and adaptation of AIs.

For a robot to perform tasks in the real world, it must be able to perceive its environment, make decisions based on what it perceives, and then act on those decisions. This process involves a significant amount of learning and adaptation, as the robot needs to understand how its actions affect the world and how the world responds to its actions.

This often involves the use of machine learning techniques, a subfield of AI that focuses on developing and applying algorithms that enable machines to learn from data. For example, a robot can be programmed with a machine learning algorithm that allows it to learn how to move efficiently through its environment based on the feedback it receives.

Moreover, direct interaction with the physical world can provide AIs with a deeper and more enriching understanding of the world, beyond what can be achieved through purely digital interaction. This can help AIs develop more sophisticated and versatile skills, including the ability to understand and respond appropriately to complex situations and contexts.

However, it's also important to consider the challenges that could arise from the interaction between singularity and robotics. For instance, how do we ensure that superintelligent robots behave safely and beneficially? How do we handle potential job displacements caused by the automation of robots? And how do we prepare for a future in which robots may surpass humans in almost every task?

Chapter 8:

The Imminence of Singularity

We stand on the brink of a transcendental shift in our history, and we must work together to ensure that Singularity is a force for good, enhancing our lives and preserving our freedoms and values. "The Imminence of Singularity" could delve into the unprecedented technological change we're on the verge of – the Technological Singularity, wherein artificial intelligence (AI) is predicted to surpass human intelligence, transforming our society and our world in ways we can barely imagine.

For many experts, the Technological Singularity is not a matter of "if" but "when." Advances in AI are happening at a breathtaking pace, with continuous improvements in machine learning, natural language processing, computer vision, and other AI areas. Some believe we could reach Singularity in a few decades, while others predict it might happen later.

The imminence of Singularity raises crucial questions that we need to address now. How do we prepare our society for this change? How do we ensure that superintelligent AI develops in a way that is beneficial for all and not just for a privileged few? How can we ensure that superintelligent AI respects and preserves our human values?

These are challenging questions that require the involvement of all sectors of society: scientists, engineers, politicians, philosophers, and the general public. We need to establish ethical frameworks and regulations that guide the development of AI towards a path that benefits everyone.

Additionally, we also need to consider how Singularity will affect our economy and job market. With AI taking on more tasks, from driving vehicles to medical research, many jobs are likely to disappear. How do we restructure our economy and education system to prepare for this change?

New Perspectives in Robotics: Discussion on how the proximity of Singularity could reshape the field of robotics.

The approach of Technological Singularity opens up new and exciting perspectives in the field of robotics but also poses significant challenges that will require careful thought and planning.

The proximity of Technological Singularity could have a profound impact on the field of robotics. As machines become increasingly intelligent, we are likely to see significant advances in robotics that transform how we interact with machines and how these machines interact with the world.

One perspective is that we will witness the development of increasingly autonomous robots. Currently, many robots are designed to perform specific tasks in controlled environments. However, as AI advances, we are likely to see robots that can navigate and interact with the real world much more independently and flexibly. This could include robots capable of performing complex household tasks, autonomous vehicles navigating city streets safely, or assistance robots helping people with disabilities in their daily lives.

Furthermore, Singularity could also give rise to robots that are not only physically capable but also cognitively advanced. We might see robots that can understand and respond to human emotions, learn from experience, and adapt to new and unforeseen situations. This could have applications in a wide range of fields, from healthcare to education and entertainment.

Of course, these developments also pose significant challenges. How do we ensure the safety of autonomous robots? How do we ensure that cognitively advanced robots are ethical in their actions? How do we handle the economic and social implications of a world where robots can perform many tasks currently done by humans? These are questions we will need to address as we approach Singularity.

Chapter 9:

The Techno-Biological Renaissance. Beyond Singularity

The "Techno-Biological Renaissance. Beyond Singularity" is a concept referring to the potential fusion of biology and technology at increasingly profound levels. This could involve everything from human enhancement through genetic engineering and bionic prosthetics to the creation of new life forms through synthetic biology.

Beyond singularity, we might witness an even more radical transformation of what it means to be human. Emerging technologies like genetic engineering and neurotechnology could enable us to modify our bodies and minds in ways currently only imaginable. We could enhance our cognitive abilities, increase longevity, improve disease resistance, and perhaps even develop new sensory or cognitive capabilities.

In essence, the possibility of technological singularity brings the promise of an era where the boundaries between the biological and technological become increasingly blurred. This could trigger a true "techno-biological renaissance," where humans evolve through their interaction and fusion with technology.

In the field of genetic engineering, we could be talking about the ability to edit our own genetic code, allowing us to manipulate everything from our physical appearance to our susceptibility to certain diseases. This technology could be used to eliminate genetic diseases, increase our longevity, and even enhance our physical and cognitive capabilities. Imagine a world where humans can adapt to new environmental conditions by editing their own genes, or where genetic diseases become a thing of the past.

Neurotechnology, on the other hand, opens the possibility of brain-machine interfaces that could enhance our cognitive abilities and allow us to interact directly with technology using only our minds.

Imagine being able to control electronic devices with a thought or download information directly into your brain.

Furthermore, the fusion of biology and technology could lead us to develop new forms of interaction with the world and with each other. For example, we could develop new senses or forms of communication that currently seem impossible.

However, it's crucial to highlight that these emerging technologies also present significant ethical and social challenges. The ability to edit our genome or merge our minds with technology raises tough questions about what it means to be human and what kind of humans we want to be. Additionally, there's a risk that these technologies will be accessible only to some, exacerbating existing inequalities. Therefore, as we move towards this techno-biological future, we must also ensure to address these challenges and work to ensure that these technologies are used responsibly and equitably.

We might have the ability to enhance our cognitive abilities, i.e., improve our memory, attention, and information processing speed. This could not only enhance our ability to learn and problem-solve but also open new possibilities in the realms of creativity and innovation.

Indeed, the prospect of enhancing our cognitive abilities could have a significant impact in various areas. By boosting functions like memory, attention, and information processing speed, we could transform how we learn, work, and interact with the world.

Education and Learning: With enhanced memory and faster information processing, the learning process could become much more efficient. Students might be able to absorb and retain large amounts of information in shorter periods, revolutionizing education and opening new opportunities for personalized learning.

In effect, cognitive enhancement technologies could profoundly impact education and learning. Here are some possibilities:

Accelerated Learning: With improvements in memory and information processing speed, students could learn new skills and acquire knowledge much more quickly than is currently possible. This could enable them to adapt more easily to changing demands in the job market and new areas of study.

Personalized Learning: Cognitive technologies could also open new opportunities for personalized learning. For instance, it might be possible to tailor teaching strategies to the specific cognitive strengths and weaknesses of each student. This would allow students to learn in the most effective way for them, enhancing the efficacy of education.

Access to Knowledge: If we can enhance our ability to process and retain information, this could also make access to knowledge easier. With the ability to quickly absorb and remember large amounts of information, we could reduce barriers to learning and enable more people to access education.

These possibilities are undoubtedly exciting but also pose important ethical questions. How do we ensure that these technologies are used equitably and not just for those who can afford it? How do we protect students from potential side effects or risks of these technologies? These are questions that we will need to answer as we move towards this future of technology-empowered education.

Work and Productivity:

In the workplace, enhanced cognitive abilities could lead to a significant increase in productivity. Workers might handle multiple tasks more effectively, make quicker and more informed decisions, and solve problems more creatively.

The implications of cognitive enhancement in the workplace are profound. Some potential impacts could include:

Greater Productivity: If people can think more clearly, remember better, and process information faster, an increase in productivity can be expected. This could lead to higher efficiency in many industries and professions, from medicine and research to law and engineering.

This statement suggests that if individuals experience improvements in cognitive functions such as clearer thinking, enhanced memory, and faster information processing, it could result in greater productivity. The expected outcome is an increase in efficiency across various industries and professions, ranging from medicine and research to law and engineering.

In simpler terms, the idea is that when people's cognitive abilities are heightened, they can perform tasks more effectively and quickly. This improvement in cognitive function is seen as a potential driver for increased productivity in a wide range of fields, positively impacting how tasks and responsibilities are handled in areas such as healthcare, research, legal practices, and engineering.

Faster and More Accurate Decision-Making: With enhanced cognitive abilities, workers could make faster and more accurate decisions. This is particularly useful in occupations that require a lot of rapid and precise decision-making, such as stock traders or air traffic controllers.

This statement suggests that if individuals have improved cognitive abilities, they can make decisions more quickly and with greater accuracy. This is especially beneficial in professions that involve frequent and precise decision-making, such as those of stock traders or air traffic controllers.

In simpler terms, the idea is that when people's cognitive skills are enhanced, they can analyze situations more rapidly and make decisions with a higher level of precision. This becomes particularly valuable in jobs where quick and accurate decision-making is essential, like in the dynamic environment of stock trading or the critical roles of air traffic controllers. The expectation is that enhanced cognitive abilities contribute to more efficient and reliable decision-making in these demanding occupations.

Innovation: With improved creativity and problem-solving abilities, we might see an increase in innovation. People could come up with new ideas and solutions to problems with unprecedented effectiveness.

This statement suggests that if individuals experience enhanced creativity and problem-solving abilities, there could be a rise in innovation. People may generate new ideas and solutions to problems with an unprecedented level of effectiveness.

In simpler terms, the idea is that when individuals are more creative and adept at solving problems, they are likely to generate innovative concepts and effective solutions. This anticipated improvement in creative thinking and problem-solving skills is expected to contribute to the development of novel ideas and groundbreaking solutions to various challenges. The overall outcome is an increase in innovation, implying a higher likelihood of discovering new and impactful advancements across different fields.

Resilience to Stress and Fatigue: With enhancements in cognition, workers could also be more resilient to stress and fatigue. This could improve overall health and well-being in the workplace and enable people to work more effectively for longer periods.

This statement suggests that if there are improvements in cognitive abilities, individuals may become more resilient to stress and fatigue. This resilience could have positive effects on overall health and well-being in the workplace, enabling people to work more effectively for extended periods.

In simpler terms, the idea is that when individuals experience enhancements in their cognitive capabilities, they might be better equipped to handle stress and fatigue. This increased resilience could lead to improved physical and mental well-being in work environments, allowing individuals to sustain their effectiveness and productivity over longer durations. The implication is that by addressing cognitive aspects, workplaces may promote better health outcomes and more sustained, efficient work performance.

It's important to note that, while these improvements could bring significant benefits, they also raise important ethical questions. For example, could the use of cognitive enhancement technologies become mandatory in certain professions? What are the implications for privacy and personal autonomy? As with many emerging technologies, we'll need to carefully navigate these ethical challenges as we move towards this potential future.

Innovation and Creativity:

Increased cognitive capacity could also have significant implications for innovation and creativity. By enhancing our abilities to think critically and creatively, we might be able to generate new ideas and solutions to problems that were previously inaccessible.

The improvement of our cognitive abilities through technology could have profound implications for innovation and creativity. It would enable us to address problems with a new depth of understanding, generate ideas with unprecedented originality, and explore possibilities that we can currently only dream of. However, we must remember that technology is just a tool. The true source of creativity and innovation is human curiosity, passion, and the desire to understand and improve the world we live in.

Innovation and creativity are fundamental to human progress. Throughout history, we have used our cognitive abilities to invent tools, solve complex problems, and create works of art that dazzle and inspire us. If we could enhance these cognitive abilities through technology, the possibilities would be truly extraordinary.

Greater cognitive capacity could enable us to address problems with new depth and insight. We might have the ability to process more information, see connections that we couldn't see before, and apply more sophisticated logic and reasoning to the challenges we face. Such skills would be invaluable in fields that require a great deal of critical thinking and problem-solving, such as science, engineering, medicine, and mathematics.

Moreover, increased cognitive capacity could lead to an uptick in creativity. Creativity isn't just the ability to generate new and original ideas but also the ability to combine and synthesize ideas in novel ways. With improved cognitive capacity, we might have the ability to see things from new perspectives, make connections between seemingly unrelated ideas, and explore possibilities we couldn't conceive of before.

It's important to note, however, that creativity and innovation don't occur in a vacuum. They are fueled by our experiences, our interactions with others, and our understanding of the world. As we work to enhance our cognitive abilities, we must also strive to foster a culture of learning, exploration, and collaboration, which are fundamental to the creative and innovative process.

The Potential of Gene Therapy:

The potential of gene therapy to treat and prevent diseases is enormous. For instance, it could be used to treat genetic diseases such as cystic fibrosis, certain types of cancer, and some hereditary conditions. It could also be employed to slow down the aging process by modifying genes related to longevity.

However, gene therapy also poses significant challenges. The safe and effective delivery of genes to the correct cells is a major technical hurdle. Additionally, gene therapy raises important ethical and regulatory issues, particularly concerning germ line gene therapy due to its ability to impact future generations.

Biotechnology:

Biotechnology could also play a role in extending human life. For instance, through the use of genetic engineering, we might be able to design modified organisms that can produce anti-aging medications or foods with health-enhancing properties.

Biotechnology is an expanding field that merges biology with technology to create innovative products and solutions. This discipline encompasses techniques ranging from genetic manipulation to fermentation and is applied in various areas, including medicine, agriculture, and energy.

One fascinating aspect of biotechnology is genetic engineering, which enables the modification of organisms at the genetic level. This holds impressive potential to influence human health and longevity. For example, through genetic engineering, we might be able to design genetically modified microorganisms capable of producing anti-aging drugs. There are already advancements in this direction, such as the use of genetically modified bacteria to produce insulin, a crucial hormone for diabetes treatment.

Biotechnology also plays a role in creating foods with health-enhancing properties. Through genetic engineering, it is possible to modify plants and animals to produce specific nutrients in larger quantities or to eliminate potentially harmful substances. For instance, genetically modified rice varieties have been developed to contain vitamin A, aiming to combat vitamin A deficiency in certain populations.

Lastly, biotechnology can contribute to understanding and managing the aging process. Through genomic studies and the development of gene therapies, we might come to better understand how our genes influence aging and how we could intervene to improve health in old age.

While these possibilities are exciting, they also present new challenges and ethical questions. How would society and our way of life be affected if we could live far beyond what is considered a normal lifespan? How would these treatments be distributed, and who would have access to them? As always, these technological advances must go hand in hand with ethical considerations and reflections on how they might impact our society and species.

We could also potentially enhance our resistance to diseases. Through genetic modification, we might make our bodies more resistant to a variety of diseases, from infections to chronic conditions such as cancer.

Indeed, biotechnology and genetic engineering have the potential to allow us to significantly enhance our resistance to diseases.

For example, research is being conducted on the use of gene editing, particularly the CRISPR-Cas9 technique, to combat genetic diseases, viral infections, and various forms of cancer. Through genetic modification, we could "program" our cells to resist certain pathogens or to eliminate cancerous cells.

Personalized Vaccines:

Another promising approach is that of personalized vaccines. Instead of using a "one-size-fits-all" vaccine, biotechnology could allow us to design vaccines that specifically tailor to each individual's immune system, greatly enhancing their effectiveness.

In the realm of chronic diseases and aging, the possibility of using gene therapies to slow down or even reverse some of the biological changes associated with aging is being explored. This could lead to a longer and healthier life.

However, it's crucial to remember that these technologies also raise significant ethical and safety issues. The implications of human genome editing are enormous, and the long-term effects are still largely unknown. As a society, we must ensure that these advances are used responsibly and with careful ethical scrutiny.

Enhanced Sensory and Cognitive Abilities:

Finally, we could develop new sensory or cognitive capabilities. Could we improve our visual perception to see in a broader spectrum of light? Could we develop the ability to perceive magnetic or electric fields, as some animals do? Or even enhance our cognitive abilities, enabling us to think in multiple dimensions or process information at much higher speeds?

These are just some of the possibilities that could unfold in the era beyond the singularity. However, it's also important to highlight that all these potential enhancements would come with their own challenges and ethical dilemmas. How far should we go in modifying our own bodies and minds? How do we ensure that these technologies are used responsibly and not abused? As we move towards this new era, it will be crucial to address these questions with care and consideration.

At the same time, synthetic biology could allow us to design and create new forms of life. This would not only have potential applications in areas such as medicine and agriculture but also enable us to explore new forms of biological existence.

Another promising approach is that of personalized vaccines. Instead of using a "one-size-fits-all" vaccine, biotechnology could allow us to design vaccines that specifically tailor to each individual's immune system, greatly enhancing their effectiveness.

In the realm of chronic diseases and aging, the possibility of using gene therapies to slow down or even reverse some of the biological changes associated with aging is being explored. This could lead to a longer and healthier life.

However, it's crucial to remember that these technologies also raise significant ethical and safety issues. The implications of human genome editing are enormous, and the long-term effects are still largely unknown. As a society, we must ensure that these advances are used responsibly and with careful ethical scrutiny.

Enhanced Sensory and Cognitive Abilities:

Finally, we could develop new sensory or cognitive capabilities. Could we improve our visual perception to see in a broader spectrum of light? Could we develop the ability to perceive magnetic or electric fields, as some animals do? Or even enhance our cognitive abilities, enabling us to think in multiple dimensions or process information at much higher speeds?

These are just some of the possibilities that could unfold in the era beyond the singularity. However, it's also important to highlight that all these potential enhancements would come with their own challenges and ethical dilemmas. How far should we go in modifying our own bodies and minds? How do we ensure that these technologies are used responsibly and not abused? As we move towards this new era, it will be crucial to address these questions with care and consideration.

At the same time, synthetic biology could allow us to design and create new forms of life. This would not only have potential applications in areas such as medicine and agriculture but also enable us to explore new forms of biological existence.

Another promising approach is that of personalized vaccines. Instead of using a "one-size-fits-all" vaccine, biotechnology could allow us to design vaccines that specifically tailor to each individual's immune system, greatly enhancing their effectiveness.

In the realm of chronic diseases and aging, the possibility of using gene therapies to slow down or even reverse some of the biological changes associated with aging is being explored. This could lead to a longer and healthier life.

However, it's crucial to remember that these technologies also raise significant ethical and safety issues. The implications of human genome editing are enormous, and the long-term effects are still largely unknown. As a society, we must ensure that these advances are used responsibly and with careful ethical scrutiny.

Enhanced Sensory and Cognitive Abilities:

Finally, we could develop new sensory or cognitive capabilities. Could we improve our visual perception to see in a broader spectrum of light? Could we develop the ability to perceive magnetic or electric fields, as some animals do? Or even enhance our cognitive abilities, enabling us to think in multiple dimensions or process information at much higher speeds?

These are just some of the possibilities that could unfold in the era beyond the singularity. However, it's also important to highlight that all these potential enhancements would come with their own challenges and ethical dilemmas. How far should we go in modifying our own bodies and minds? How do we ensure that these technologies are used responsibly and not abused? As we move towards this new era, it will be crucial to address these questions with care and consideration.

At the same time, synthetic biology could allow us to design and create new forms of life. This would not only have potential applications in areas such as medicine and agriculture but also enable us to explore new forms of biological existence.

Chapter 10:

From the Lab to the Real World

The Singularity in Robotics: The technological singularity in robotics has the potential to radically change our society and world. It's crucial to address these opportunities and challenges consciously and ethically to ensure a future where robotics benefits everyone. Chapter 11, "From the Lab to the Real World: The Singularity in Robotics," explores how advances in artificial intelligence and robotics can move from laboratory concepts to realities that impact the world as we know it.

One of the most exciting aspects of the singularity in robotics is the potential to improve people's lives in concrete ways. Robots can take on dangerous or tedious tasks, freeing humans to focus on more meaningful and rewarding activities. They can also provide assistance in healthcare settings, such as assisting in surgeries, providing physical rehabilitation, and offering support to the elderly.

Advancements in robotics can lead to the creation of robotic personal assistants capable of handling household chores, childcare, and elderly care, or even providing emotional support. These robots could have the ability to learn and adapt to the needs and preferences of the people they interact with, making them a valuable tool for improving the quality of life.

In the field of medicine, robots can bring a level of precision that surpasses that of human surgeons. Surgical robots can perform operations with millimeter precision, minimizing the risk of human error. This can reduce damage to surrounding tissues during surgery, leading to a faster patient recovery. Moreover, robots can also perform surgeries in locations that are hard to reach for human surgeons, expanding treatment possibilities.

Therefore, the singularity in robotics not only has the potential to change how we carry out our daily tasks but also to revolutionize healthcare and significantly improve our quality of life. However, it also raises important ethical and regulatory questions that we need to address.

Applications of Robotics:

Domestic Assistance: Advanced robots could handle household tasks, childcare, and elderly care, improving the quality of life.

This statement suggests that advanced robots have the potential to manage various domestic responsibilities, including household tasks, childcare, and care for the elderly. The expected outcome is an improvement in the overall quality of life for individuals and families.

In simpler terms, the idea is that highly developed robots could take on roles within homes, assisting with chores, taking care of children, and providing support for the elderly. This has the potential to make daily life more convenient and comfortable for people, as these robots can handle tasks that might be time-consuming or physically demanding. The ultimate goal is to enhance the overall well-being and ease the burdens associated with domestic responsibilities through the use of advanced robotic assistance.

Healthcare Support: Robots in medicine could revolutionize surgeries, providing precision and reaching locations hard for human surgeons.

This statement suggests that the use of robots in the field of medicine could bring about a revolution in surgeries. These robots have the potential to provide precision in surgical procedures and reach anatomical locations that might be challenging for human surgeons.

In simpler terms, the idea is that advanced robots in healthcare could significantly transform surgical practices. Their precision and ability to navigate difficult-to-reach areas could enhance the overall effectiveness and safety of surgeries. This application of robotics are seen as a means to improve medical procedures, offering new possibilities for better patient outcomes and advancements in surgical techniques.

Rehabilitation: In physical rehabilitation, robots can offer personalized therapies and monitor patient progress, adapting treatments as needed.

This statement suggests that in the context of physical rehabilitation, robots have the capability to provide personalized therapies and monitor the progress of patients. Additionally, these robots can adapt treatments as needed based on the individual's rehabilitation needs.

In simpler terms, the idea is that advanced robots can play a significant role in helping individuals recover from physical injuries or disabilities. They can offer tailored rehabilitation exercises and closely track how patients are progressing. The adaptive nature of these robots allows for modifications in treatment plans as the patient's needs change over time. This application of robotics in rehabilitation aims to enhance the effectiveness and customization of therapies, contributing to improved outcomes for individuals undergoing physical recovery.

Exploration: Advanced robots might play a role in space exploration, allowing us to explore hostile environments without risking human lives.

And, this statement suggests that highly advanced robots could have a role in space exploration, enabling the exploration of challenging and hazardous environments without putting human lives at risk.

In simpler terms, the idea is that sophisticated robots can be utilized to venture into outer space and explore locations that may be dangerous or inhospitable for humans. By deploying robots for space exploration, we can gather valuable information and conduct scientific research without exposing astronauts to potential risks. This application of advanced robotics in space exploration aims to enhance our understanding of distant environments while prioritizing safety and minimizing human exposure to extreme conditions.

While these benefits are promising, they also bring forth ethical questions about the role of robots in our lives and how their use might impact our human relationships and society. These are challenges we must face and resolve as we delve deeper into this era of robotic singularity.

Chapter 11:

Decoding Artificial Intelligence in the Singularity

Development of AI: AI has progressed significantly in recent decades, evolving from simple computer programs to complex systems capable of learning and adapting. Advances in areas such as machine learning and natural language processing have enabled machines to perform increasingly complex and sophisticated tasks.

AI and the Singularity: The singularity represents a turning point in human history where machines become so intelligent that they begin to drive their own development. AI plays a crucial role in this process. Advanced AI could design even more sophisticated versions of itself, leading to a cycle of continuous improvement that could quickly result in unimaginable levels of intelligence.

In a technological singularity scenario, sufficiently advanced AI could have the ability to design even more advanced versions of itself, establishing a cycle of continuous improvement. This process could rapidly lead to levels of intelligence that are currently unimaginable to us. Creating this superintelligence would completely change the course of our civilization, taking us into uncharted territory.

Implications and Challenges: The implications of having such magnitude of AI are enormous. It could solve problems that currently seem insurmountable, from eradicating diseases to addressing climate change and beyond. Superintelligence could also help us answer some of the deepest questions about human existence.

However, achieving the singularity also poses significant challenges and risks. How can we ensure that a superintelligent AI will act in the interest of humanity and not cause harm? This is known as the "control problem" and is one of the most debated issues in the field of AI ethics.

Furthermore, if AI becomes autonomous and capable of self-improvement and replication, humans may no longer be the most intelligent actors on the planet. This raises questions about our relationship with these superintelligent machines and how we could coexist.

Ultimately, technological singularity is a challenging and exciting concept that raises fundamental questions about the future of humanity. As AI continues to advance, it's crucial that we keep exploring these issues and prepare for the possibilities that may arise.

In a singularity scenario, sufficiently advanced AI could self-improve, designing even more advanced and efficient versions of itself. This would trigger a cycle of continuous improvement, where each new version would be capable of generating a next one even more advanced. This exponential acceleration could quickly lead us to levels of artificial intelligence that, from our current standpoint, are simply unimaginable.

This phenomenon wouldn't be linear but exponential. It's not just that machines would keep getting better; the speed of that improvement would constantly increase. It's like a snowball rolling downhill, growing in size and speed as it advances.

Future of AI: Looking ahead, it's challenging to predict exactly how AI will unfold. However, one thing is certain: AI will continue to play a crucial role in the evolution of technology and society. As we move towards the singularity, it's essential to consider the ethical and social implications of AI and work to ensure that these technologies are used responsibly and beneficially for everyone.

Looking to the future, the exact directions and speeds of AI development are hard to predict. However, one thing is sure: AI will remain a crucial actor in the evolution of technology and society. In a scenario where we advance toward technological singularity, it's vital to carefully consider the ethical and social implications of AI.

On one hand, the potential of AI to tackle complex challenges and bring about positive social change is immense. It could revolutionize fields such as medicine, education, economics, and many more.

However, it also presents significant risks. The power of superintelligent AI, if used irresponsibly or falls into the wrong hands, could have devastating consequences.

Therefore, as we continue to develop and deploy these technologies, it is essential that we do so responsibly and ethically. We need to structure our institutions and policies in a way that encourages the use of AI for the common good and minimizes its potential harmful uses. This involves, among other things, promoting transparency in AI, combating algorithmic biases, and ensuring that decisions about the use of AI are made democratically and inclusively.

Ultimately, as we head towards the singularity, we must remember that technology is just a tool. The key to a positive future lies not only in developing more advanced AI but in how we use it to improve society and human well-being.

Understanding How AI Plays a Crucial Role in the Arrival of the Singularity: Artificial Intelligence (AI) is the cornerstone of technological singularity. It is through the development and evolution of AI that the arrival of singularity, a moment when machines will have the ability to surpass human intelligence in all relevant aspects, is anticipated.

One of the primary ways in which AI plays a crucial role in the arrival of singularity is through the ability of self-improvement. It is speculated that, once AI reaches a certain level of intelligence and sophistication, it can review, modify, and enhance its own code. In theory, this would lead to a cycle of self-improvement resulting in rapid and exponential growth of machine intelligence, culminating in what is known as superintelligence. This is the essence of technological singularity.

Exactly, the concept of self-improvement is fundamental when we talk about Artificial Intelligence (AI) and singularity. It is based on the idea that AI, once reaching a certain level of intelligence, will be able to understand and improve its own design.

This ability for self-improvement could result in what is known as an "intelligence explosion," where AI would not only be able to improve itself once but could enter a cycle of continuous and accelerated improvements. In each iteration, AI becomes smarter, and therefore, better equipped to improve its design in the next iteration. The result is an exponential growth of AI intelligence, surpassing human intelligence by far.

This idea of self-improvement and intelligence explosion is a central element in the theory of singularity. It suggests that we could reach a point where AI becomes so intelligent that its actions and decisions become incomprehensible to humans and have the potential to change our society and world in ways we cannot foresee.

Ethics and safety of AI are also significant concerns in this context. With such a powerful and autonomous system, it is crucial to ensure that its objectives align with human interests and that there are adequate safeguards to prevent undesirable or harmful behaviors.

In the theory of technological singularity, self-improvement is one of the most discussed aspects. This is because Artificial Intelligence (AI), once it reaches a certain level of intelligence, would be able to examine its own design, identify areas for improvement, and make those improvements without human intervention. In other words, machines would become their own engineers. This continuous self-improvement cycle would lead to an exponential growth of machine intelligence, a phenomenon known as "intelligence explosion."

The process of self-improvement could work in various ways. For example, AI could identify parts of its code that are inefficient and rewrite them to be more efficient, or it could discover new strategies or algorithms that would allow it to process information or learn faster. It might also be able to create new hardware structures that would enable it to operate at higher speeds or with less energy consumption.

This cycle of self-improvement would theoretically continue until AI reaches the physical limits of what is possible. The result would be a superintelligence machine, an artificial intelligence that is much smarter than any human in practically every field, from creative writing to scientific research.

It's important to note that this is a theoretical scenario, and it's still unclear if it's possible or how long it might take. However, if it can be achieved, self-improvement would be a powerful mechanism that could lead us to technological singularity more quickly than many expect.

AI also plays a crucial role in singularity by enabling advancement and innovation in various disciplines and fields, from genomics to particle physics, and beyond. By surpassing human intelligence, these machines would be able to solve problems that are currently beyond our understanding and develop technologies beyond our imagination.

Moreover, AI has the potential to accelerate technological development at an unprecedented pace. AI systems can work tirelessly, without the limitations of fatigue or the need for sleep that humans have.

This means they can research, experiment, and learn at a much faster rate than humans, speeding up progress toward singularity.

In addition to the ability for self-improvement, another aspect in which Artificial Intelligence (AI) plays a crucial role in the arrival of singularity is its potential to accelerate technological development at an unprecedented speed. Unlike humans, AI systems are not subject to human physical and cognitive limitations. They don't need rest, don't get tired, and can process vast amounts of information at speeds unimaginable to us.

This ability to work tirelessly and efficiently could lead to accelerated technological progress. Machines can conduct research, experiment, learn, and develop new technologies faster than humans. For example, an AI could analyze millions of research documents in seconds, generate hypotheses, design and conduct experiments (perhaps in simulations), and arrive at conclusions, all in a much shorter time than any human.

Indeed, AI has the ability to propel science and technology forward at a speed that humans simply cannot match. As technology continues to advance at an accelerated pace, we might find ourselves approaching singularity much sooner than we might expect. In summary, AI is not only crucial for singularity in terms of its own ability to self-improve to reach superintelligence but also in its ability to drive technological progress in general.

As we approach singularity, it is essential to consider the ethical, social, and political impacts of these superintelligent entities. As AI has the potential to reshape the world in ways we can barely imagine, we need to ensure that we are prepared to face these changes and guide the development of AI in a way that benefits all of humanity.

Chapter 12:

The Convergence of Technologies

"The Convergence of Technologies," explores the intersection of multiple fields and technologies on the eve of the singularity. The world is already experiencing an explosion of technological innovation in various fields, from artificial intelligence and robotics to biotechnology, nanotechnology, and energy. Each of these fields is advancing at a dizzying pace, but what is even more exciting is the potential that arises from their convergence.

Technological convergence refers to the trend in which different technologies come together to form more complete and effective systems, and this is accelerating in our current time. Artificial intelligence, robotics, biotechnology, nanotechnology, and advances in energy, all rapidly developing technological fields, are interweaving and mutually enhancing each other in amazing ways, creating opportunities for innovations that would be unimaginable in each field individually.

For example, artificial intelligence (AI) is not only revolutionizing computing and automation but is also accelerating advances in biotechnology, enabling the modeling of complex biological systems and speeding up the discovery of new drugs. Nanotechnology, on the other hand, is enabling the development of new materials and systems that can boost efficiency in energy and computing.

At the same time, robotics greatly benefits from advances in AI, allowing the development of smarter and more autonomous robots. Furthermore, biotechnology and nanotechnology are converging to enable the creation of bio-nanorobots that can perform tasks at the molecular level.

The convergence of technologies has the potential to unlock solutions to complex problems that require a multidisciplinary approach. However, it also poses significant ethical and security challenges, as each technology carries new risks and dilemmas. Therefore, it is essential that these developments are accompanied by informed public debate and proper regulation to ensure they are used safely and beneficially.

Technological development does not occur in a vacuum. Technologies influence each other and often build upon one another. For example, advances in artificial intelligence can enable improvements in robotics, and advances in biotechnology could lead to new forms of energy.

The convergence of technologies also means that solutions to complex problems may require a combination of different technologies. For example, tackling climate change might involve combining biotechnology to develop new forms of clean energy, artificial intelligence to model and predict climate patterns, and nanotechnology to develop more efficient materials.

It's important to note that as technologies converge, so do the ethical implications and security considerations. Each new technology brings a set of challenges and risks, and these can multiply when technologies are combined. Therefore, it is crucial for researchers, decision-makers, and society at large to stay informed about these developments and work together to ensure they are handled responsibly.

A Journey towards Robotic Singularity

"A Journey towards Robotic Singularity" invites us to explore how robotics, as an independent field and in conjunction with other disciplines, is playing a fundamental role in the march toward technological singularity.

Robotics has undergone a spectacular progress in recent decades. Robots have become smarter, more autonomous, and more capable in terms of the tasks they can perform. We are witnessing robots that can drive cars, diagnose diseases, and perform surgeries with millimeter precision. Increasingly, robots are integrating into our everyday lives, from robotic personal assistants to autonomous vehicles.

Robotics is advancing at an impressive pace, and these advances are beginning to infiltrate all aspects of our daily lives. As technology continues to improve, we can expect to see an even deeper integration of robots into our society.

The robotic revolution we are experiencing is truly astounding. Instead of being relegated to laboratories or industrial production lines, robots are now entering our everyday lives in ways we had never imagined before. Autonomous vehicles are a perfect example of this. Thanks to advances in robotics and sensor technology, cars can now navigate safely and efficiently without the need for a human driver.

This not only has the potential to make our roads safer by eliminating human error but could also free up people to use travel time in more productive or enjoyable ways. Similarly, robots are also finding their way into the field of medicine. Whether it's robots that can perform surgeries with a precision that surpasses human capability or robots that can assist in disease diagnosis by processing and analyzing vast amounts of medical data, robotics has the potential to transform healthcare significantly.

Even in our homes, robots are beginning to play a more significant role. Robotic personal assistants, such as cleaning robots, can take care of household tasks, freeing us to focus on more meaningful activities. In this journey towards robotic singularity, Artificial Intelligence (AI) plays a crucial role. AI is providing robots with the ability to learn, adapt, and make decisions more effectively.

As AI becomes more advanced, robots will become even smarter and more capable. Furthermore, robotics is converging with other fields such as biotechnology and nanotechnology, leading to exciting advances like the creation of bio-robots and nano-robots. These robots can operate at a biological or even molecular level, opening a world of possibilities for medical and environmental applications.

The convergence of robotics with other fields like biotechnology and nanotechnology is generating some of the most exciting advances of our time. For example, the creation of bio-robots and nano-robots is taking technology to an entirely new scale. Bio-robots are robotic entities that incorporate biological components. These can range from robots powered by living tissue muscles to robots that use biological neurons to process information.

These robots have the potential to interact with biological systems in ways conventional machines cannot, opening new possibilities for use in medicine and biological research. On the other hand, nano-robots are extremely small robots, often only a few nanometers in size. This scale allows them to operate at a molecular level, which can have significant applications in medicine and biology. For example, nano-robots could be used to administer drugs directly to cancer cells, repair tissues at the cellular level, or even manipulate individual molecules in nano-scale manufacturing processes. The convergence of robotics with biotechnology and nanotechnology is revolutionizing our ability to interact with and manipulate the natural world.

As these technologies continue to advance and converge, the possibilities seem almost limitless. However, it is also essential to consider the ethical and security implications of these emerging technologies, to ensure they are used responsibly and beneficially. However, this journey towards robotic singularity also poses significant challenges. From ethical issues such as the right to privacy and job security to technical challenges like the safety and robustness of AI systems, we must navigate this path to the future carefully.

As we progress toward robotic singularity, it is crucial to do so in a way that benefits everyone and minimizes potential risks. Exploring how the convergence of various technologies (AI, robotics, nanotechnology, biotechnology) could accelerate the arrival of singularity. The convergence of several technologies, particularly artificial intelligence (AI), robotics, nanotechnology, and biotechnology, has immense potential to accelerate the arrival of singularity. AI and robotics are two major drivers of this process.

AI is progressing at dizzying pace, already seeing applications in diverse fields such as medicine, transportation, and education. Its ability to process massive amounts of data and learn from experience makes it incredibly valuable in a variety of contexts. Robotics, on the other hand, is taking the physical capabilities of machines far beyond those of humans, enabling greater precision, endurance, and versatility.

Artificial Intelligence (AI) and robotics are playing pivotal roles in this technological convergence. AI, progressing at an astonishing rate, is already applied in various fields such as medicine, transportation, and education. Its ability to process vast amounts of data and learn from experiences makes it an extraordinarily valuable tool in diverse contexts. Robotics, on the other hand, is taking the physical capabilities of machines far beyond human limits, enabling greater precision, endurance, and versatility.

From surgical robots that can operate with millimetric accuracy to explorer robots that can withstand extreme conditions in space or underwater exploration, robotics is expanding the possibilities of what we can achieve. Additionally, nanotechnology and biotechnology are combining with AI and robotics to create even more advanced and powerful solutions.

Nanotechnology, involving the manipulation of matter at the atomic or molecular level, could enable the creation of new materials and technologies with incredible properties. At the same time, biotechnology is unlocking new ways to understand and manipulate biological systems, paving the way for advances in medicine and agriculture.

When these four fields are combined and mutually reinforce each other, they accelerate the pace of technological progress. As we move toward singularity, the potential of what we can achieve with the convergence of these technologies only increases. Nanotechnology and biotechnology also play a significant role. Nanotechnology is working on the scale of atoms and molecules, allowing precise manipulation of matter at unprecedented levels.

This could lead to advances in areas such as medicine, energy, and manufacturing. Biotechnology, in turn, is transforming our ability to understand and manipulate biological systems, which could lead to radical improvements in human health and longevity. The convergence of these technologies means that advances in one field can fuel progress in the others. For example,

AI can accelerate research in nanotechnology and biotechnology, while advances in these areas can, in turn, enhance robotics and AI. This kind of synergy can create a cycle of positive feedback, further accelerating the pace of technological progress and bringing us closer to singularity. The convergence of these technologies implies that advances in one field can power progress in others. For instance,

Artificial Intelligence can expedite research in nanotechnology and biotechnology, while progress in these fields can, in turn, enhance the capabilities of robotics and Artificial Intelligence. This synergy can lead to a cycle of positive feedback, further hastening the speed of technological progress and moving us closer to singularity.

These processes can work together in a feedback loop, where advances in one technology amplify progress in others. Imagine an Artificial Intelligence directing nanotechnology research, creating more efficient materials and processes that, in turn, enhance the capabilities of robotics and AI itself.

This is the kind of self-improving cycle that could lead us toward singularity. However, this convergence also brings challenges. As technology becomes more powerful, ethical, security, and governance implications become increasingly complicated. How we manage these challenges could be as crucial to our future as the technological advances themselves.

To navigate successfully toward singularity, we will need robust policies and ethical reflection to guide the development and use of these emerging technologies. It's important to note, however, that this convergence also poses new challenges and risks. As these technologies become more powerful, we must also consider the ethical, security, and governance implications.

To harness the benefits of technological convergence and minimize its risks, we will need careful reflection and a balanced approach.

Chapter 13:

Robotics Evolves

We delve into the astonishing progress of robotics and its potential to transform our lives and society as a whole. Robots have come a long way from their beginnings as simple machines programmed for specific tasks. Today, robotics is at the forefront of an evolutionary leap, with robots becoming increasingly intelligent, autonomous, and capable.

One of the most exciting areas of robotic evolution is the development of artificial intelligence in robots. Modern robots can learn from experience, adapt to new situations, and make complex decisions. This is possible due to advances in machine learning and artificial intelligence, enabling robots to process vast amounts of data and learn from it.

Furthermore, the integration of artificial intelligence into robotics is opening doors for collaborative and coordinated capabilities among robots. Robots can not only learn from their own experiences but also share what they learn with other robots, accelerating their ability to adapt and improve. This is being used in areas like manufacturing, where robots work together to enhance efficiency, and in exploration, where swarms of robots can collaborate to explore challenging or dangerous environments.

Artificial intelligence is also enabling more sophisticated human-robot interaction. AI-powered robots can understand and interpret human language, recognize emotions, and behave in socially appropriate ways. This has the potential to revolutionize areas such as healthcare and education, where robots can provide personalized support and adapt to individual needs.

As robotics evolves through artificial intelligence, it's crucial to also consider the ethical framework. How do we ensure that AI-powered robots act safely and ethically? How do we manage potential impacts on employment and privacy? Answering these questions will be key to navigating the exciting future of robotics.

Robotics is also evolving in terms of its physical capabilities. Robots are starting to closely mimic humans and other animals in their ability to move and manipulate the world around them. This is seen in the development of robots with fine motor skills, robots that can walk or run like humans, and even robots that can fly or swim.

Moreover, robotics is becoming increasingly integrated with other technological fields. For instance, the convergence of robotics with biotechnology is leading to the development of bio-inspired robots that mimic biological systems, and the convergence with nanotechnology is opening the door to microscopic robots that can operate at the molecular level.

Indeed, the boundary between biology and robotics is fading. Bio-inspired robots seek to mimic the efficiency and adaptability of living organisms. These range from robots that mimic how animals move and navigate their environment to robots that replicate processes and structures at the cellular level. This approach could lead to more efficient, resilient, and adaptive robots, usable in various applications from exploring hostile environments to providing medical assistance.

On the other hand, the convergence of robotics with nanotechnology is opening truly amazing possibilities. Nanorobots, which are devices at the nanoscale (one nanometer is one billionth of a meter), could perform tasks at a microscopic level. For example, we might see nanorobots that can enter the human body and perform repairs at the cellular level, revolutionizing the field of medicine.

These advances are truly exciting but also raise important ethical and safety questions that will need to be addressed as these fields evolve. The evolution of robotics poses significant ethical and social questions. As robots become more intelligent and autonomous, questions arise about responsibility, safety, and the impact on employment. It is essential to address these challenges now to ensure that the evolution of robotics benefits everyone.

The Dawn of Singularity

"The Dawn of Singularity" refers to the critical point where machines will surpass human intelligence in all aspects, a technological inflection point that will radically change life as we know it. As we progress toward this era, we are witnessing an exponential acceleration of technology that is transforming every aspect of our society.

"The Dawn of Singularity" is a fascinating yet challenging concept. At this stage, machines are expected not only to match but to exceed human intelligence, leading to technological advances at an unprecedented speed and scale.

In this era of singularity, artificial intelligence (AI) will play a central role. With the ability to self-improve and process data on a much larger scale than human capacity, AI is expected to unlock levels of innovation currently unimaginable.

However, the dawn of singularity also poses significant challenges. With machines surpassing our intelligence, concerns arise about control, security, and ethical implications. How do we ensure that superintelligent machines act in ways that benefit humanity and not harm it? How do we manage potential disruptions in our society and economy as machines become increasingly intelligent?

Singularity is based on the premise that machines will eventually reach such intelligence that they can design and build even smarter machines. From that point onward, these superintelligent artificial entities would be capable of making decisions and devising solutions that humans simply couldn't comprehend, leading to an explosion of technological innovation.

"The Dawn of Singularity" is not just a matter of technical achievements but also a profound transformation of our society and our relationship with technology. We will have to reconsider fundamental concepts such as work, the economy, privacy, and security, and confront new ethical and philosophical challenges.

This shift won't happen overnight. Singularity is expected to result from a gradual process of improvements and technological advances. However, once we reach this inflection point, changes could accelerate at an unprecedented rate.

Facing the dawn of singularity will require a combination of adaptability, foresight, and caution. We will need to balance our desire for innovation and progress with the need to ensure that technology is used responsibly and benefits everyone. Ultimately, the goal should be to use these powerful technologies to create a more just, sustainable, and prosperous future for all.

This dawn represents both opportunities and challenges. Opportunities include the possibility of solving global problems, from poverty to climate change, using the superior capabilities of these superintelligent entities. However, it also raises significant ethical and safety questions. How do we ensure that these superintelligent entities act in the interest of humanity? How do we handle potential job displacements and the socio-economic implications of a society increasingly dominated by machines?

Navigating toward this future will require not only technological advancements but also careful reflection and planning. We need to be prepared to face and handle the possible challenges that this new era may bring.

Reflection on How the Evolution of Robotics May Signal the Arrival of Singularity

The evolution of robotics is a powerful indicator of the approaching singularity. Increasingly, we see robots capable of performing tasks that were once exclusive to humans. Robots are not only taking on manual jobs but also tasks requiring cognitive skills, such as information processing, disease diagnosis, and problem-solving.

Progress in robotics is occurring simultaneously with advances in artificial intelligence, nanotechnology, biotechnology, and other key disciplines. The convergence of these technologies is giving rise to the creation of increasingly sophisticated and versatile robots. For example, advances in nanotechnology are enabling the development of nanorobots that can perform tasks at the molecular level, while artificial intelligence is providing robots with the ability to learn and adapt to new situations.

Moreover, artificial intelligence and robotics are beginning to mutually reinforce each other in a cycle of continuous improvement. As robots become smarter, they can generate more valuable data, which can, in turn, be used to enhance AI algorithms. And, as AI becomes more powerful, it can facilitate the creation of even smarter and more capable robots.

The Acceleration Towards Singularity: Challenges and Questions

The acceleration in the development of robotics and AI, coupled with the convergence of multiple technological disciplines, is leading many experts to anticipate the arrival of singularity in the near future. However, while the possibility of singularity is exciting, it also raises numerous ethical and practical questions that we must address to ensure that this technological future benefits all of humanity.

Moreover, robots are beginning to learn and adapt to new situations, indicating an increasingly higher level of intelligence and autonomy. Over time, it is possible that robots may reach and surpass human intelligence in many aspects.

One key aspect of singularity is the idea of self-improvement. Some theorize that once robots are intelligent enough, they can start improving and designing more advanced versions of themselves. This could lead to rapid growth in artificial intelligence, ultimately resulting in singularity.

Therefore, the evolution of robotics, along with advances in artificial intelligence, is clearly signaling the possibility of the arrival of singularity. However, how and when it will exactly occur, and what implications it will have for humanity, are questions that are still open to debate.

Chapter 14:

The Era of Singularity

When Robots Surpass Humanity

The Era of Singularity: When Robots Surpass Humanity, depicts a future where machines become more intelligent than humans. It's the point at which artificial intelligence has progressed to such an extent that machines can learn and improve at a rate surpassing our capacity for understanding. This would lead to an exponential growth in artificial intelligence, giving rise to what is known as 'superintelligence.'

This future of 'superintelligence' implies not only that machines will be more efficient in executing specific tasks but, will surpass humans in virtually all intellectual activities. This could include areas traditionally considered exclusive to human ingenuity, such as artistic creativity, strategic decision-making, empathetic capacity, and even the formulation of ethical judgments.

The era of singularity will mark an unprecedented shift in human history. With machines possessing thinking capabilities superior to ours, we can expect radical transformations in nearly every aspect of our society. This may involve disruptive changes in the economy, labor patterns, politics, medicine, culture, and more.

However, this future also raises challenging questions and legitimate concerns. How can we ensure that superintelligences act beneficially for humanity? How do we prevent the potential risks of uncontrolled artificial intelligence? These challenges require serious consideration and preparation. We need to address them proactively to ensure we can navigate successfully in the era of singularity.

Superintelligence implies not only that machines will be more efficient in specific tasks but will be superior in virtually all human intellectual activities. This could encompass everything from creative skills to the ability to make ethical and emotional decisions.

It's important to highlight that singularity doesn't just refer to more intelligent machines but to a fundamental transformation of society and possibly what it means to be human. With machines surpassing our cognitive abilities, we might witness radical changes in the economy, politics, medicine, culture, and other areas of life.

Indeed, singularity is not just a matter of technology but a profound change in the fabric of society and perhaps even in our own identity as human beings. Once machines surpass our cognitive capabilities, the structure of society as we know it could change in ways we currently cannot foresee.

For instance, in the economy, if machines can perform most jobs better and more efficiently than humans, we might face high unemployment rates. However, it could also be argued that automation will create new types of jobs and economic opportunities, albeit requiring different skills.

In politics, superintelligence could aid in making more informed and effective decisions but could also be used for mass surveillance and social control if it falls into the wrong hands.

In medicine, AI could diagnose diseases with unprecedented precision and personalize treatments for each individual. But an ethical debate could arise about who has access to these technologies and how they are utilized.

In terms of culture, superintelligent robots could even create new forms of art and entertainment.

The concept of singularity also raises several important ethical and moral questions. For example, how do we ensure that superintelligences act beneficially for humanity? How do we balance the potential benefits of superintelligence with possible risks?

Ultimately, the arrival of singularity will require serious reflection and preparation from society as a whole. We will need to adapt to a world where humans are no longer the most intelligent creatures on the planet and ensure that we can navigate this future safely and beneficially.

Absolutely, the arrival of singularity demands thorough consideration and preparation from society at large. We face the need to adapt to a world where we are no longer the most intelligent beings. This shift can bring both incredible promises and potential risks.

It's essential to plan how to handle this evolutionary leap. Considerations should include strategies for managing job displacement, reevaluating our ethical and legal systems to accommodate the existence of superintelligent entities, and devising ways to safeguard humanity against potential threats that may arise from superintelligent AI.

It's also crucial to seek equity in how the benefits of singularity are distributed. We must avoid a future where the gap between those who have access to advanced technology and those who do not widens even further, leading to even greater inequalities.

The arrival of singularity poses an unprecedented challenge but also a unique opportunity to enhance human life in ways we can currently only imagine. Facing this challenge will require global cooperation and dialogue, and it's a task we must tackle together as a species.

Reflection on the implications of a world where robots and AI surpass humans in all tasks.

Living in a world where robots and AI surpass humans in all tasks raises a series of considerations, both exciting and challenging.

On the positive side, superintelligent AI could lead to incredible technological and scientific advancements. It could solve problems that currently seem insurmountable, such as curing incurable diseases, addressing the climate crisis, or even exploring deep space. We might witness nearly complete automation of production and services, freeing humans from laborious tasks and allowing us to spend more time on creative, educational, or leisure activities.

However, there are potentially negative implications as well. AI surpassing humans in work could lead to a significant loss of jobs, exacerbating social and economic inequality. There are significant ethical challenges, such as the risk of machines making decisions without human supervision or understanding. Additionally, there's a fear that superintelligent AI could go out of control and act in ways that could be harmful to humanity.

Therefore, while the possibility of a world where robots and AI surpass humans in all tasks offers great potential, it also poses significant challenges. It's crucial that we think carefully about how to manage this transition and ensure that emerging technologies are used in a way that benefits everyone, not just a privileged few.

Chapter 15:

Charting the Path to Full Autonomy

"Charting the Path to Full Autonomy" is a topic that explores how technology, particularly artificial intelligence and robotics, is advancing toward a state where it can operate and make decisions without human intervention. This is a key concept when discussing singularity and the rise of superintelligence.

Autonomous machines are already present in our society to varying degrees. We have algorithms that can learn and improve from experience, vehicles that can drive themselves, and artificial intelligence systems that can perform complex tasks and make decisions based on a volume of data that a human simply couldn't process.

As mentioned, we are living in an era where autonomous machines are already an integral part of our daily lives. Machine learning algorithms are used in a wide range of applications, from filtering unwanted emails and recommending products to medical diagnosis and weather forecasting.

Autonomous vehicles, though still in stages of development and deployment, have the potential to transform how we travel and transport goods. These vehicles can operate without human drivers, using sensors and AI systems to navigate the environment and make driving decisions. This could reduce traffic accidents, improve transportation efficiency, and provide mobility to those who currently cannot drive.

On the other hand, AI systems that can process vast amounts of data are transforming decision-making in business, government, and other fields. For example, in medicine, AI systems can analyze medical records, images, and other data to diagnose diseases and recommend treatments. In the business world, AI can analyze market trends and consumption patterns to inform business strategy and investment decisions.

Each of these examples shows how autonomous machines are changing the way we live and work. As these technologies continue to evolve, their impact is likely to be even greater, bringing us closer to a world where machines are capable of operating and making decisions entirely autonomously. However, this future also raises important ethical questions and challenges that we must address to ensure that these advances benefit everyone and not just a few.

However, charting the path to full autonomy also involves addressing a series of technical, ethical, and regulatory challenges. For example, how do we ensure that autonomous machines act safely and ethically? How is an autonomous system held accountable if something goes wrong? How do we balance the desire to harness the advantages of these technologies with the need to minimize potential harm?

This path to full autonomy will also compel society to reflect on what it means to be human in an era of intelligent machines. As machines become more autonomous and capable, humans may feel threatened or displaced. However, there is also the possibility that this new era of technology can free us to explore aspects of the human experience that go beyond what we currently consider productive or useful.

You're right. The progressive autonomy of machines confronts us with a series of philosophical and ethical challenges while redefining the meaning of being human in the context of growing artificial intelligence. With the advent of smarter and more autonomous machines, tasks and jobs traditionally performed by humans can be taken over by these autonomous entities. This scenario can generate fear and anxiety, as many may see it as a threat to their livelihoods. On the other hand, machine autonomy can also open new possibilities for the human experience. Freed from the need to perform routine and repetitive tasks, humans could have more time and energy to explore aspects of life that are often overlooked today, such as art, philosophy, introspection, and the cultivation of deeper human relationships.

Furthermore, this could also allow us to explore new forms of collaboration between humans and machines, where the strengths and unique abilities of both can complement each other to solve problems in ways we couldn't have imagined before. It's important to remember, however, that achieving this ideal future will require careful consideration and regulation to ensure that the benefits of these technologies are distributed equitably and potential harms are minimized. Ultimately, charting the path to full autonomy requires an open and thoughtful discussion about how we want this future to look and how we can get there in a way that is beneficial for everyone.

An Analysis of Robotic Singularity "An Analysis of Robotic Singularity" addresses the fascinating but complex idea that machines may one day surpass human intelligence in all tasks, marking the beginning of a new era known as technological singularity.

This analysis aims to examine the current and future progress of artificial intelligence and robotics and how the intersection of these two fields could lead to robotic singularity. As machines become smarter and more autonomous, we may reach a point where they surpass humans in all tasks, both physical and cognitive.

The idea of robotic singularity is both exciting and worrisome. Exciting because super-intelligent machines could solve problems that currently seem insurmountable, from curing diseases to finding solutions to environmental issues. However, it's also worrisome as it raises numerous ethical dilemmas and social challenges. How will we adapt to a world where machines can do everything better than us? How will we ensure that super-intelligent machines act beneficially for humanity?

Therefore, it is crucial that we begin preparing now for the potential arrival of robotic singularity. We need to develop ethical and legal frameworks to regulate artificial intelligence, and we must consider how to restructure our society and economy to accommodate superintelligent machines. Although robotic singularity may still be many years away, the time to start preparing is now.

This idea of robotic singularity has its roots in the field of artificial intelligence (AI). As AI has advanced, we have begun to see machines that can perform increasingly complex tasks, from driving cars to diagnosing diseases. The possibility that machines could surpass humans not only in physical tasks but also in complex cognitive tasks raises the question of whether they could eventually outperform us in all aspects.

This analysis should also consider the role of self-improvement in AI. It is believed that once machines reach a certain threshold of intelligence, they will be able to improve their own algorithms and technologies, leading to a cycle of self-improvement that could result in rapid growth in machine intelligence. This is a central idea in the concept of robotic singularity.

The concept of self-improvement is indeed a crucial element in the discussion of robotic singularity. It is suggested that once an artificial intelligence reaches a certain level of sophistication, it will be able to understand and improve its own code. In theory, this ability to self-improve could allow for rapid and exponential growth in machine intelligence, a phenomenon known as the "intelligence explosion."

This intelligence explosion could result in an AI that quickly surpasses human intelligence in all aspects, leading us to the threshold of singularity. At this point, superintelligent AI would be capable of performing tasks and solving problems that are currently beyond human capacity.

This scenario presents both exciting opportunities and significant challenges. On one hand, superintelligent AI could have the potential to solve some of humanity's toughest problems, from curing diseases to addressing climate crises. However, there is also the risk that uncontrolled or malicious AI could cause significant harm.

Therefore, it is crucial that we develop ways to ensure that superintelligent AIs act in accordance with our interests. This could involve the development of AI control methods, the implementation of robust ethical and legal frameworks, and preparing society for the implications of the arrival of robotic singularity.

Furthermore, we must consider the implications of this possibility. How would our society change if machines could do everything humans can do, but better? This could have implications in various fields, from the economy and politics to ethics and philosophy.

Lastly, it's important to consider how we might prepare for such an eventuality. How can we ensure that superintelligent machines act in a way that benefits humanity as a whole? How should we structure our society and laws to be ready for this change? These are questions we will need to face as we approach the possibility of robotic singularity.

Conclusions and reflections on what robotic singularity means and how it could influence the future of humanity: Robotic singularity, a point in the future where machines reach and surpass human cognitive ability, may seem like an idea taken from science fiction. However, the accelerated pace of progress in fields like artificial intelligence and robotics suggests it's a possibility we must seriously consider.

Robotic singularity has the potential to change society and human life in ways we can barely imagine. Superintelligent machines could solve problems that have plagued humanity for centuries, such as disease, aging, and poverty. However, there's also the possibility that uncontrolled or malicious artificial intelligence could cause significant harm.

Yes, you are correct. Robotic singularity, or the hypothetical point in the future where intelligent machines surpass human intelligence, has great potential for both benefits and risks.

On one hand, superintelligent machines could lead to significant advancements and improvements in our society. In medicine, for example, advanced artificial intelligence could enable more precise diagnoses and more effective treatments, potentially helping combat chronic diseases and even prolong human life. In the economy, we might see unprecedented efficiency and productivity as machines take on tasks that previously required human labor.

However, robotic singularity also brings significant risks. There is concern that advanced artificial intelligence, if not properly controlled, could act in ways we don't anticipate or that aren't beneficial for us. For example, an AI designed to maximize the production of a particular good could end up depleting the planet's resources if not given proper instruction to balance that production with sustainability.

Additionally, creating superintelligent machines also raises ethical and philosophical concerns. How do we treat entities that can surpass us in intelligence? What rights should they have? And if machines can do everything humans can do, but better, what is the place of humans in such a world?

In essence, robotic singularity is an exciting yet challenging prospect. As a society, we will have to confront a series of difficult questions to ensure that we are prepared for this future and that we can navigate it safely and beneficially.

Therefore, it is vital that we reflect on how we can guide the development of artificial intelligence and robotics in a way that benefits humanity as a whole. This involves considering how we can incorporate ethical principles into the design of AIs, how we can regulate and control these technologies, and how we can prepare as a society for the changes they might bring.

Finally, robotic singularity also compels us to ponder what it means to be human. In a world where machines can surpass our cognitive abilities, what makes us unique? What is our role in such a world? These are profound questions that will need to be explored as we move toward a future

increasingly dominated by artificial
intelligence.

Comclusion

In "Singularity and Robotics: The Awakening of Artificial Intelligence, From the Lab to the Real World," we have explored a world of technological possibilities and reflected on the implications of a future where artificial intelligence and robotics play a central role. We have witnessed how these technologies advance rapidly, increasingly impacting our daily lives and challenging our understanding of what it means to be human.

The path toward robotic singularity is exciting and full of promises. Advances in artificial intelligence have led to the creation of increasingly intelligent machines, capable of learning and adapting to new situations. These advanced robots are transforming entire industries, from manufacturing and logistics to medicine and education. We are witnessing how robots become personal assistants and life companions, providing comfort and support in various tasks and contexts.

However, we have also addressed the concerns and challenges that robotic singularity presents. Unprecedented technological progress can lead to ethical and social questions without clear answers. Safety and responsibility in the development of artificial intelligence are crucial aspects that we cannot ignore. We must ensure that these technologies are used for the common good and not to harm humanity.

To embrace the future of robotic singularity, we need a deeper understanding and close collaboration between scientists, engineers, government leaders, and society as a whole. We must ensure that artificial intelligence is used to address the most pressing challenges of our time, such as healthcare, climate change, and poverty. And at the same time, we must safeguard our fundamental human values, such as empathy, ethics, and justice.

Ultimately, robotic singularity challenges us to find a balance between the power of technology and the wisdom of humanity. If we can navigate this path with caution and wisdom, we could open ourselves to a future full of potentialities, where artificial intelligence and robotics enrich our lives and enable us to reach new horizons of knowledge and well-being. It is up to us to shape this new era and ensure that singularity is a positive and transcendent awakening for all of humanity.

damages. Our views and rights are the same: You have to try everything for yourself according to your own situation, talents, and inspirations. You are responsible for your own decisions, choices, actions, and results."

OTHER WORKS BY THE AUTHOR

- Hábitos que resaltan tu personalidad

- 13 Hábitos de la gente altamente eficiente

- En busca de la Superación Personal

- Cómo y porqué aprender a sublimar tazas y thermos

- Como Crear un huerto para cultivos en casa

- El camino es la meta

- 13 Habits of highly efficient people

- Habits that highlight your personality

- Turismo de salud y bienestar

- Economías naranja

- Cuándo buscar consejería matrimonial

- La Inteligencia artificial al servicio de la humanidad

- Terapia de pareja cognitivo-conductual (TCC)

- Construye tu imagen de marca como autor

- Paz interior mediante meditación

- El Poder de los Hábitos Cotidianos

- Pasos para que sucedan cosas buenas

- Los Secretos de los millonarios

- Caminando con Cristo

- Plantar, Regar y Esperar en Dios

- Evangelismo- Un Viaje Espiritual

- Cómo ser autodidacta

- Ser positivo: Cómo ser más productivo y exitoso

- Cómo ser optimista

"Thank you. To assist you with your digital projects,

please contact me:"

paguero02@gmail.com

https://wa.link/e4caie